Everyday Creative Play

• •

Everyday Creative Play

· ·

Simple Fun Things You Can Do to Help Your Young Child Learn

Lisa R. Church

Fairview Press   *Minneapolis*

Published by Fairview Press, 2450 Riverside Avenue South, Minneapolis, MN 55454.

Library of Congress Cataloging-in-Publication Data
    Church, Lisa R., 1960–
        Everyday creative play : simple fun things you can do to help your young child learn / Lisa R. Church.
           p.   cm.
           ISBN 1-57749-069-X (alk. paper)
           1. Education, Preschool--Activity programs.
           2. Education, Preschool--Parent participation.
           3. Play. I. Title.
           372.21--dc21   98-2508
                                  CIP

First Printing: April 1998
Printed in the United States of America
02 01 00 99 98   7 6 5 4 3 2 1

Cover design: Laurie Duren
Interior illustrations: Marilyn Mets

Publisher's Note: Fairview Press publishes books and other materials related to the subjects of social and family issues. Its publications, including *Everyday Creative Play*, do not necessarily reflect the philosophy of Fairview Health Services. For a free current catalog of Fairview Press titles, please call toll-free 1-800-544-8207. Or visit our Web site at www.Press.Fairview.org.

Contents

A Child's Request

Teach me some more,
We can't be done yet!
You get the paper,
I'll get my paint set.

Ask me some questions.
Read me a book.
Tell me a story,
Then let me help cook.

Let's get out a puzzle,
Or go for a walk.
The patio's quiet—
Let's just sit and talk.

You know what I like,
You've taught me so well.
Put down those papers,
Let's sit for a spell.

We'll dream about pirates
And kittens and birds.
We'll practice our numbers
Then write down some words.

Oh, teach me some more,
Our day is not through.
There's nothing more special
Than being with you.

For Tommi Ann, Alexander, and Allison . . .
You gave me the joy of being a Mom.
No matter what I achieve in life,
you will always be my proudest accomplishments.
I love you.
Mom

Introduction

A child's life is filled with wonder, excitement, and curiosity. Every day is a new adventure—from big words to new foods to weird-looking bugs. What a thrill to wake up each morning, not quite knowing what to expect from the world! What temptations lie ahead? What challenges will arise? Without this wide-eyed anticipation, this innate need to learn, there would be no innocence of childhood.

Imagine what a child could accomplish if we nourished his or her quest for knowledge. Where would this knowledge lead? What could the child become? There are children everywhere who are taking the potential they are given and running with it, eager to get the most out of each new experience. These children do not attend special schools or programs; they are taught by the most important mentors in the world—their parents.

Mom and Dad may have created life; now they have a chance to make life creative. All it requires is a commitment to make time for the child, to foster his or her love of life whenever an opportunity arises. This does not mean setting aside an hour each day to "play school." It means taking advantage of each and every learning opportunity. It's that simple.

Simple? Yes. Easy? No. You are your child's first teacher. Helping your little one reach his or her full potential takes patience, creativity, and your own quest for the simple pleasures in life. Once you make the commitment, you'll find that learning opportunities arise naturally. Helping your child discover the world will become second nature.

Anyone can teach children at home—working parents, stay-at-home parents, grandparents, even baby-sitters. You don't have to be a certified public school teacher to open up the world of learning for a child. You need only show an interest in his or her capabilities.

Chapter 1 discusses a child's overall health and well-being. After all, healthy children who are content with family life are likely to succeed in school. But just when we thought we had the basics down, our children discovered television or the candy aisle at the supermarket, and parenting got harder. Moms and dads question their parenting decisions every day: "Am I feeding my child the right kinds of food?" "Is my style of discipline appropriate and beneficial to my child?" "Is my little one getting enough exercise?" Chapter 1 addresses these concerns while offering a little insight into a child's world.

Chapters 2 through 8 introduce activities that are specifically designed to stimulate a young child's desire to learn. With your guidance, your little one will acquire the skills necessary to prepare him or her for success in school. Moreover, you and your child will grow closer as you live, laugh, and learn together through these early years. The strength of this bond is the most precious gift you will ever have to offer.

Each subject in this book—reading, writing, numbers, community, science, and health—lists activities that can take place at home, on the town, or in the car. Refer to this section for suggestions to help your child learn specific skills. Together, you can make boring car rides and long rainy days into lively family affairs. Moreover, you and your child will rediscover exciting areas in town, turning libraries, museums, and parks into learning sanctuaries.

So grasp the learning opportunities as they come. Create an interest in new subjects. Capture your child's excitement about learning, and nurture it. Fill your child's early years with wonder and anticipation. Bring some creative play into your every day.

Chapter 1

Getting Started

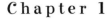

From the moment your child is born, it is up to you to make the most of every day. Prepare your youngster for school, but always remember that there is more to life than academics. Fill every day with new experiences, exciting adventures, and plenty of hugs and praise. Involve your youngster in music, exercise, and thoughtful decision making. Visit the theater, join the Scouts, hang out at the playground. Appreciate your time together.

You will notice substantial improvement in motor skills and coordination throughout these early years. Running, jumping, catching, and throwing a ball will enhance your child's large motor skills, while more intricate activities—writing with sidewalk chalk, playing in the sandbox, and gardening with small tools—will improve his or her small motor skills. Both are necessary for coordination, balance, and good physical health. Take every opportunity to practice these skills, and incorporate them in your lessons whenever possible.

When it comes to teaching children, creating excitement is half the battle. If your little one sees that all learning is worthwhile, the child will have a head start in school. Not every lesson will be a barrel of laughs, of course: Learning to tie a shoe can be frustrating and difficult, but if your youngster anticipates success, his or her patience will grow.

There will be many failures in a child's early years, and children need to learn that quitting is simply not an option. Success only comes with practice. Whether your child fails or succeeds, offer plenty of praise and encouragement. If your youngster believes that he or she will succeed eventually, the child will be motivated to keep trying.

Once a child gets his or her first taste of success, an "I can do it myself!" attitude will follow. They will want to dress themselves, feed themselves, and pour a carton of milk into a tiny glass by themselves. Try to be patient.

If you're in a hurry, it can be frustrating to wait for a little one to put on his or her shoes. Rather than thwart your youngster's blossoming independence, try to allow him or her enough time to get ready before you leave. This will reduce last-minute stress, relieve the temptation to do the job yourself, and allow you to reach your destination on time.

Once a child completes a difficult task, such as making the bed, he or she will feel an overwhelming sense of pride. Praise your child—and resist the urge to pull back the covers and remake the bed. In your little one's eyes, the bed is perfect. Let the child wallow in the glory. Does it really matter if the sheets hang longer on one side? Compliment your little one warmly, remembering that one day it will be a battle to get your child to make his or her bed. Enjoy the help while you've got it.

Chores

The word "housework" conjures up images of laundry machines, dirty dishes, and unmopped floors. Yuck! Who wants to do chores?

Children, that's who.

When kids make the bed, they're as pleased as punch with their accomplishment. They'll *beg* to help wash the dishes. They love pulling clothes out of the dryer, and many will even scrub the toilet if you let them. Why do we continue to abuse ourselves when we have little maids and butlers running around free of charge?

Most of the time, it's because they don't do a very good job.

NEWS FLASH! If kids enjoy doing chores, *let them.* They don't see chores as drudgery. Chores are opportunities to prove that they're growing up. Let them pitch in whenever they can—they won't do the job as well as you, but does it really matter most of the time?

As you demonstrate how chores are done, don't forget to explain why. If the child understands that we need to do laundry so we have clean clothes, and we need to mow the grass so we can play in the yard, your youngster will be even more eager to help out. Let your little one pursue that sense of accomplishment. Elicit the child's help often, and give plenty of praise and encouragement in return.

Little Chores for Little People

Dust Away

Give your child his or her own dust cloth. Spray the cloth and let your youngster polish cupboards and wooden furniture to his or her heart's content. (Do not allow children to spray the polish by themselves—they could get it in their eyes.)

Setting the Table

As you arrange the plates and glassware, let your child place the napkins and silverware around the table. Meals will be more enjoyable for everyone if the child helps with preparation.

Laundry Duty

Youngsters can help sort the lights and darks, pair up socks fresh from the dryer, and deliver clean clothes to the appropriate rooms. Kids also provide an extra pair of hands for folding sheets and towels.

Tidy Up

A simple chore like this can take up a good part of the day if you do it by yourself. By the time you've picked up stray toys, shoes, and magazines, the mess has started all over again. Instead of doing it on your own, elicit your youngster's help. Have a race to see how many personal belongings the two of you can find and put away in five minutes. Show your child that you can get twice as much work done together as you can alone. That leaves more time to play!

Neatness Counts

Let children designate a place to keep their toys, games, and puzzles. Remind them to hang up their coats and take off their shoes when they come indoors. When they finish playing with one toy, encourage them to put it away before taking out a new one.

Vacuum Partners

You can run the vacuum cleaner as your youngster rescues (and puts away) the toys that are in your path.

Better yet, give your little one a hand-held vacuum cleaner. The child will be happy to sweep the entryway or bathroom, and it saves you the trouble of doing it yourself later.

Get Cooking!

Children love to help cook, so get them in on greasing pans, measuring flour, or simply opening a package of rolls.

After-Dinner Help

Although your little one probably can't reach the sink, he or she can carry dishes to the counter, load the dishwasher, or collect the silverware.

Little Chores for Little People

Little Chores for Little People

Bedroom Business

A child's bedroom is his or her personal domain, so encourage your youngster to take charge of its appearance. Establish a morning routine as soon as possible.

Young children can put away their pajamas and make the bed. Older children can take on a few more chores. If they get used to managing their room early on, tidiness will become second nature as time goes by (hopefully).

A Special Arrangement

Move decorations or pieces of furniture to give your living room a different look every now and then. Ask your child to help determine where objects should go. Better yet, allow the youngster to rearrange toys, pictures, or books in his or her bedroom. This will encourage your little one to take pride in neatness and personal belongings.

Outdoor Chores

Kids can pick up toys, put away bikes, or help with the gardening and yard work. Buy child-size tools and let your little ones rake leaves, pull weeds, and water flowers.

Hobbies

Somewhere between the ages of two and five, children discover that they like some things better than others. They begin to show preferences—favorite toys, favorite books, favorite foods, and so forth. Their parents guide them in their choices, but youngsters begin to speak for themselves.

One way to channel this newfound independence is to steer your child toward a hobby. Hobbies allow children to collect, research, and enjoy something that interests them. Hobbies help build new skills, boost self-esteem, and encourage a child's independence. If your little one shows an interest in a particular hobby, offer to help research the topic or contribute to your youngster's collection. Your child will be thrilled to see that you share an interest in his or her favorite subject.

Some children discover their own hobbies at an early age. These are the kids who bring home rocks, leaves, bugs, and anything else that can fit in their pockets. Other children need a little guidance and gentle persuasion. If a child loves to draw, encourage his or her artwork. Supply colored pencils, markers, and plenty of paper. Introduce the little one to charcoal and finger paints. There are tons of fun and interesting hobbies out there—build on your child's interests and see how your son or daughter responds.

Hobbies

Collections

Children collect everything from pennies to rocks to feathers. Some collections cost money, however, so you might encourage children to save and pay for their collections themselves. Tell friends and relatives about their hobbies, too—hobby items make wonderful birthday and holiday gifts.

Sewing

Sewing is a hobby that can be started at a very young age. Punch holes in a paper plate to form a design or picture, then give your child a piece of yarn to lace through the holes. Once he or she masters a few of these homemade cards, let your child try cards purchased from the craft store. After that, move on to a sheet of canvas with a plastic needle and yarn, then a real needle with thread.

Gardening

From the moment they see water squirt from a hose, many children are fascinated with gardening and yard work. Every time you visit the garden, teach your child something new. Explain the names of tools, flowers, and vegetables. Demonstrate how to pull weeds, water plants, and harvest crops. Your child will learn to appreciate the beauty of nature—as well as the food it yields.

Hobbies

Sports

A fascination with sports may overtake your little one at any time. Sports teach discipline, cooperation, self-control, and teamwork. If your youngster shows enthusiasm for a particular sport, help him or her get more involved. Watch sports on television, attend games together, or allow your youngster to join a team in the area.

Art

If sketching and painting are your youngster's greatest joys, keep plenty of paper and art materials on hand. Display your child's works proudly and encourage his or her efforts. Keep sketch pads in the car and bring them along to the doctor's office, hair salon, or anyplace else that would require a long wait.

Crafts

Children who like to draw, paint, or sketch often enjoy other crafts as well. Purchase yarn, glue, scissors, glitter, play dough, and construction paper. Designate a workspace where kids can make a mess and store their materials.

Hobbies

Cooking

Most children enjoy helping out in the kitchen. If they can help select recipes, plan meals, and prepare the food, they might even discover a passion for cooking. Choose projects that your child can do somewhat independently. You'll need to take charge of the stove and microwave, of course, but let your youngster do as much as possible. Kids can decorate cookies, make cold sandwiches, or build ice cream sundaes, for example. You might even let your little one concoct his or her own recipes from time to time. (Try to sample the ones that look edible.) Given the proper encouragement, your youngster may turn out to be quite a little chef.

Bird Watching

Feed the birds in the backyard. Have your child put out a variety of seeds and bread crumbs to attract several different species, then gather everyone around to watch. Purchase a bird book suitable for your child and look up your sightings together. Keep a list of all the different birds you see at home and away.

Hobbies

Flea Markets

Traipsing through flea markets and junk stores could turn your child into an antique lover. Visit yard sales and thrift shops, too. Your child may develop an appreciation for history as he or she learns more about relics from past generations.

Jewelry Making

This is another hobby that kids can start at a young age. Let them begin with simple projects—pins made out of felt or hairbands made from elastic. Before long, they'll want to spend hours stringing together beads to make bracelets and necklaces.

Nature

Investigate the great outdoors together and take note of your child's interests. Read about insects, animals, trees, and geology. Your child may wish to pursue one of these subjects, or he or she might discover an entirely different path altogether.

Storytelling

As you might expect, storytelling comes quite naturally to many children. Tall tales form effortlessly on their lips, revealing new exaggerations with every retelling. Offer to write down the story as your child dictates, and encourage your little one to add details and refine plots. Believe it or not, many writers start out this way.

Television as an Educational Tool

Television has gotten a bad rap over the years. TV sex and violence are prevalent, and we hear more four-letter words on family sitcoms than ever before. Nevertheless, if television is used responsibly, children can actually benefit from watching it.

Television programs can spark a little one's imagination and creativity. Your son or daughter will see things on TV that he or she has never seen before. Naturally, the child will want to imitate characters or draw scenes from different shows. You don't want your youngster learning violent actions or nasty words, but if you are careful to monitor what he or she watches, you should have few problems.

When your little one wants to watch television, check the TV guide. There will probably be at least one show designed for young viewers. If there isn't, help your child find something else to do. This may require a little work on your part, but it's better than having your youngster turn on a violent movie or a talk show about adultery.

Cartoons may seem harmless enough, but these, too, can be violent and inappropriate. Don't assume that animated shows are suitable for your youngster. There are many, many cartoons that you will want to view before nodding your approval. Make an effort to preview these programs—it will be well worth your trouble in the long run.

Try to watch television together so you can be there to answer your child's questions. You might even use ideas from each show to teach your youngster about new topics. For example, if Big Bird talked about the number 3 this morning, reinforce the lesson by counting in threes for the rest of the day.

Of course, not every show has to have an educational theme. But every show will teach your child something new. Select your programs wisely.

Good programs can introduce your little one to new topics, creating an interest where there was none before. Animal shows, for example, can teach kids about wildlife, endangered species, and common house pets. Help your youngster follow up on these topics. Check out nature books from the library, make a big book about animals, or encourage your child to make up a story about an endangered species.

Many programs are designed for young children. *Sesame Street, Barney and Friends,* and *Mr. Roger's Neighborhood* should be a part of every child's life. As corny as they may seem to grown-ups, the songs, games, and characters on these shows enthrall kids. Find the programs your child likes best, and insist on healthy viewing habits:

- **Limit TV viewing time.** Sitting for long periods at a time isn't healthy for children. Kids need to play and run and expend energy, so don't turn your little one into a couch potato. And remember, you are your child's best role model. If your youngster sees you plopped in an easy chair for several hours a day, he or she will see nothing wrong with doing the same. Give your child options: "Mark, there's a good program on at 6:30 about polar bears and another at 7:30 about cats. Which would you like to watch tonight?" Both are appropriate, but do you really want your youngster sitting in front of the TV for two hours in the evening? Consider videotaping one of the programs and saving it for another day.

- **Turn off the TV when you're not watching it.** When your child is playing, reading, or participating in another activity, teach your youngster to turn off the television. If the house seems too quiet, turn on the radio or put a tape in your child's tape recorder.

- **Never let television take the place of books.** Both books and TV can teach positive values and important information, but nothing can compare to a good book. Books can be read together—slowly. You can stop from time to time to question the child for comprehension. Best of all, your child will revel in the one-on-one attention.

By the time the average child starts school in the United States, he or she will have viewed 4,000 hours of television. Hopefully, your child will fall well below this average. With a little effort, you and your child can develop a positive viewing routine that will enhance your youngster's learning and enjoyment. Television can be a wonderful resource. Use common sense and good judgment to make the most of this educational tool.

Socialization

It is impossible to be with your youngster all the time—at some point, you will have to entrust the child to a teacher, baby-sitter, or relative. By the time your little one enters school, he or she should feel comfortable with another adult in charge, otherwise the child may react with fear or resentment. Therefore, it's a good idea to help your youngster feel safe and secure with other caregivers from the start.

Give children an opportunity to make adult acquaintances. Take them to your workplace, highlight their week with a meal at a fancy "grown-up" restaurant, and introduce them to friends that you pass on the street. As children spend a little more time among grown-ups, they will begin to feel more responsible and independent.

When your child enters school, he or she will be expected to show respect for teachers and other classmates, so begin teaching etiquette at an early age. Tell your little one that the teacher is in charge, like Mom and Dad are when the child is at home. Baby-sitters, relatives, and grown-up friends all deserve the same respect.

At school, many children find themselves in a group situation for the first time. Most are accustomed to getting their own way, especially if they are the only child in the family. They must be taught how to share, take turns, and be quiet. Unless they learn to get along with other children, they may not be invited to join in the fun.

Give your little one a head start with group manners. Go to the playground, visit the library at story time, attend a children's matinee, or let your youngster take swimming lessons. The more your child practices large-group manners, the easier it will be for him or her to adapt to school.

Neighborhood play groups are another option. Invite three or four kids and their parents to your place for a little get-together. The children can play and have snacks while the parents share their adventures in parenting. By the end of the afternoon, your youngster will have hosted his or her first party. Next month, it will be another child's turn to host. You can meet at a park, restaurant, bowling alley—any place that makes your get-togethers fun and simple.

As children become more comfortable with group relations, conflicts are sure to arise. This is where parents need to bite their tongue and blend into the background. As hard as this may seem, it is essential to allow youngsters an opportunity to resolve conflicts and disagreements by themselves. Your child will not always have a parent hovering nearby to solve arguments and appoint winners. Children need to learn how to cope with little crises on their own. Of course, if they begin to hit or throw objects, an adult needs to step in and take control. Otherwise, resist the urge to take charge and let the kids handle it. You may be surprised at how well things work out.

Listen to the conversation that follows the squabble. Do the children continue to argue? Does your child cry? Does he or she get angry and call the other children names? Your mild-mannered little Tommy may shock the pants off you when he swears at his playmates, so try to expect the unexpected.

Many parents are confused and embarrassed when their meek little boy or girl grabs a toy away from another child or gets physical with a playmate when things don't go his or her way. These things will happen. Don't punish your youngster by keeping him or her away from other children—this would deprive the child of an opportunity to practice rules and good manners. Instead, remove your son or daughter from the situation and discuss the problem rationally. Help your child understand that his or her behavior was inappropriate.

When you get home, role-play different scenarios that could occur while your child is playing with friends. "Karen, let's pretend I'm a new friend of yours and I want your teddy bear. I want it so bad that I hit you when you won't give it to me. What do you do?" Give your child time to process his or her answer and act out the role. Afterward, discuss your child's reaction. If it wasn't exactly what you had hoped for ("I'd punch him back!"), then introduce more appropriate strategies that would help to resolve the problem. This might be a good time to start teaching self-control and alternative methods of venting anger. Be patient with your child. After all, we grown-ups have had a lifetime of practice, and we still make mistakes sometimes.

As you role-play these scenarios, let your child be the friend while you be your child. If you pretend to act mean, your child will see how unbecoming it is. The child may also gain a little insight into the lives of his or her friends. For example, your little one might discover that some families can't afford to buy their children expensive toys. He or she will begin to understand that everyone is different. Appreciating these differences will help your youngster be a better friend to others.

Preschool

If your youngster is three or four years old, he or she may be ready to attend preschool. Preschool is not a prerequisite for kindergarten, however, and there is no need to enroll your child just because all your friends are doing it. If you prepare your child at home, your youngster can be ready for kindergarten with or without preschool experience.

Preschool is an excellent opportunity to expose your youngster to other children, but again, you can give your child plenty of opportunities to make friends through play groups, library story times, peewee sports teams, dance lessons, and many other activities.

There are several issues to consider when deciding whether to send your child to preschool. Will it put a strain on your budget? Will it make your mornings too hectic? Will your child be able to adjust to the amount of time he or she would spend away from home?

If you decide to send your child to preschool, check the school thoroughly before enrolling. Don't rely on the school's reputation or comments made by other parents. A preschool that is excellent for one child may be unsuitable for another. Investigate the playground, facilities, and teachers before making your decision. Trust your instincts. If something doesn't feel right, it's not the right school for your child. With a little effort, you will find a suitable preschool where your child can learn, have fun, and make new friends.

Learning Styles

No two children are alike—behaviors, likes, and dislikes vary enormously, even among siblings. Naturally, different children have different learning styles.

For example, Pam learns by doing. She will listen to verbal directions, but she only seems to understand when she tries things on her own. Pam is a "hands on" child—she loves to touch things and explore, and she gets fidgety if she sits still for too long.

Don, on the other hand, learns best by listening. He feels comfortable hearing what someone has to say, then using that information later. It doesn't seem important for him to "practice" what he has just heard.

Ginger learns best by repeating the information she has just heard and then asking questions to make sure she fully comprehends the material.

There are many different learning styles. By observing how your child learns best, you can present information in a way that will peak his or her interest and understanding.

Once the child feels comfortable with basic skills, such as counting or identifying letters of the alphabet, he or she will want to explore these subjects further. This, of course, requires some effort and preparation on the parent's part.

Supplies

There's no need to turn your home into an art supply store, but you will want to keep some of the basics on hand—crayons, pencils, stapler, tape, glue stick, paint brushes, play dough, water colors, construction paper, and child-safe scissors. You might also collect materials that will come in handy for creative projects. Yarn, beads, seashells, cardboard boxes, empty paper towel rolls, wallpaper scraps—anything a child might find unique and interesting is worth saving. Keep these materials in a box in the garage or basement, and let your child contribute to this box from time to time. When your youngster brings home rocks, leaves, marbles, and feathers, save them for future projects. Imagine children's delight when they learn that they may not only keep these little treasures, but showcase them in a project later on!

Scissors are a difficult tool for young children. Buy a pair that opens and closes easily, has a blunt end, and isn't sharp enough to cut your child. Let your little one practice cutting scrap paper before trying to cut along a line. Hold the paper as the child cuts until he or she can hold it alone.

Glue sticks also require a bit of instruction. Teach your youngster how to pop off the top and carefully rotate the glue upward. Be sure your child remembers to rotate the glue back down again before putting the lid back on. Teach the child to listen for the little click that indicates the lid is on tight so the glue won't dry out.

As your child embarks on each new learning adventure, he or she will need plenty of assistance. It's easier to teach your child to use materials correctly from the start than to correct poorly acquired skills later on.

Work Area

Some children work well at a desk, others do better sprawled out on their bed or in the middle of the living room floor. Some need perfect silence, others thrive with loud music or television. All kids are different, so observe your child to learn what works best.

And let's not forget, we're talking about little kids here! Learning is supposed to be fun and exciting, so make your child's space something to look forward to.

Many learning activities require a lot of space. An ideal work area might be the floor in a room where materials won't be in the way. When children are unable to finish a project in one sitting, they can leave their materials out and return to the project later.

Incidentally, some parents insist that their children put all their materials away at bedtime, but this only discourages children from participating in lengthy activities. Imagine what happens when children realize that every time they start a project, they have to hurry up and finish or the project will be torn apart and put away. How can children feel good about their accomplishments if they are rarely allowed to see their projects through to the end? If a child is building the best castle ever, but he or she is called to lunch, let the child leave the blocks out. When the castle is finished, watch for that pride of accomplishment gleaming in the little one's eyes.

When your child wants to write, cut, or glue materials, you will need a table instead of a desk or floor. Give your child room to spread out. Accidents are going to happen, of course, so choose an area where occasional splatters and dumps won't be a major problem. Kitchens are nice because of linoleum floors and nearby sinks, but carpeted areas are fine as long as you put down an old rug or plastic mat first.

Keep supplies and utensils in a nearby box with a lid, and strive to keep the space uncluttered when it's not in use. Your child will be more likely to sit down and begin a project if the materials are always available.

If the weather is nice, set up a workspace outdoors. Try the yard, the porch, or the garage. Better yet, let your youngster work at a small, portable picnic table. When your child wants to draw, paint, or play with clay, simply move the table to a good spot and let the mess begin. But remember, materials and supplies can be ruined if they are left out overnight.

Before your child starts his or her next project, decide on a work area that is best for both of you. The playing, the learning, and the fun will take place no matter where you are, so give yourself a break and limit the risks of stained carpets, cluttered kitchen tables, and unhappy children.

Motivation

It's easy to motivate a child to learn—make learning fun! "Sit down, we're going to practice numbers," is not what children want to hear when it's time to learn how to count. Instead, try "You can have three pieces of candy from the jar." You'll be amazed at how quickly a child can learn to count to three! This works when you're doing chores, too. "Please pick up six blocks, then I'll pick up the rest." With just one sentence, you will have taught your child about counting, sharing, and putting away toys. Activities like these will teach your youngster the skills he or she needs for school, giving your child a healthy start. Make learning fun and interesting, and your child's enthusiasm will carry over into his or her academic life.

The next several chapters offer suggestions for introducing your child to different subjects. Try one or two activities to start with, then move on to others. Before you know it, life-long learning will become a reality instead of just a goal.

Chapter 2

Reading

Reading is the single most important activity you can do with your child. In fact, books teach a child more than all of his or her other activities combined. They bring adventure, information, new perspectives—and every time you snuggle up to read with your little one, you give that child your undivided attention. You send the message loud and clear: "You are worthwhile, and I love you."

Read big, colorful picture books to your child. For babies (and toddlers who still put everything in their mouth), use books made from cloth or plastic. Let kids pore over the pictures and make up their own dialogue. Then move on to simple books with one or two words per page. Soon your child will be able to "read" these books on his or her own.

Everything is new to children, so choose a variety of books and let your little one discover his or her favorites. If your child has a hard time sitting still for story time, try shorter books with colorful pictures, or bring home subjects that will spark your child's interest. And remember, you are your child's role model. The more your little one sees you read, the more he or she will want to read, too.

When you read to your child, you give meaning to the concepts "beginning," "middle," and "end." You expose your little one to different people, places, and ideas. Your child will learn not only to comprehend stories, but to discuss them.

Expose your little one to many, many books and make them available throughout your house. Read to your child, then invite him or her to "read" to you. Praise your little one as he or she describes the pictures and makes up a story.

For a child to read, he or she must be read to. Fill your child's life with games, puzzles, and other activities, but always make reading your number one priority. Cuddle up with your child and a stack of books, and let the learning begin. If only everything were this simple!

At Home

Bedtime Stories

Make books part of your bedtime routine. That fifteen to thirty minutes of undivided attention will mean the world to your child, and before you know it, you'll find your little one reading right along with you.

Homemade Picture Books

Paste magazine pictures onto paper or have your child draw special illustrations to create a picture book of his or her own. Let the child tell the story from the pictures while you write down his or her words underneath. Finally, make attractive covers out of construction paper and tie the pages together with colorful yarn.

Magazines

Give your child a magazine subscription of his or her very own. How exciting it is to get a magazine in the mail every month! Your youngster will eagerly await each new issue.

Newspapers

Read the comics together, or summarize interesting articles for your child. Who says news is boring?

At Home

Poetry and Nursery Rhymes

Kids love the sing-songy rhythm of poems, and they'll have the words memorized before you know it.

Record a Story

Tape-record yourself reading a children's book. Your little one will be thrilled to hear a familiar voice retell his or her favorite story again and again.

A Special Keepsake

Tape-record your child retelling a story. It may not contain the exact same words as the book, but it will be an original masterpiece, and the cassette will make a great keepsake for parents or grandparents.

New Readers for Old Stories

When Grandma or Aunt Charlotte come to visit, hand them a children's book! New readers can liven up old stories, and your child will love the attention.

Puppet Show

Buy a durable puppet to help you read, or make a few puppets of your own. Help your child design puppets out of socks or paper bags. Some books even come with a character puppet—check your local bookstore.

Nametags

When children see the same words over and over again, they eventually memorize them. Introduce your child to "sight words" by putting nametags on simple objects in his or her bedroom or playroom. For example: BED, DOLL, and DOOR.

Talk It Up

Talk about all the different things your son or daughter will learn to read. Get your child excited about reading! As soon as he or she learns how, the child will be able to read cereal boxes, television commercials, instructions to games—anything the child wants to!

Big Books for Little Kids

Big books are much larger than standard children's books, boasting great big pictures and large type. Kids love reading big books just for the novelty of it.

Buy one or two big books to keep on hand, or help your youngster make them at home. Paste drawings or magazine pictures onto large paper, and let your child tell the story as you write down the words. The end product will be BIG, and your child will want to read it over and over again.

At Home

A New Twist

Kids love to read the same books over and over again, so if Mom or Dad needs a little diversity, simply close the book and change the ending! Tell your little one that *this* time the book will end differently and ask what he or she thinks should happen next. If you're feeling particularly creative, make up your own ending and see how quickly your little one catches on!

Dream Vacation

Before you go on vacation, pick up a few books or pamphlets about your destination. Reading to little ones about what they will see and do relieves anxiety and helps build excitement.

Storytelling

Retell the classics for your child in simple terms, or make up stories your child might enjoy. Better yet, encourage your little one to make up stories to tell to *you*.

Books Come Alive

Encourage your little one to "become" his or her favorite character. You may need to do a little role-playing to help your child understand what you mean, but your little one should catch on quickly.

All the World Is a Stage

Gather up some costumes, make a few props, set the scene, and have your youngster role-play his or her favorite story. Let your little one put on the play for guests, family, or the neighborhood kids.

Book Clubs

Join a children's book club! Kids are thrilled to receive new books in the mail every month, books especially for them. Book clubs are a wonderful way to encourage a child's interest in reading.

Filling the Bookshelves

Reading is more fun when there's a big selection of books to choose from! Bookshelves can never be too full, and as long as free public libraries exist, there's no excuse for reading the same old stories.

A Family Affair

Have older children read to younger ones, and let younger kids share their own stories. Make sure the grown-ups get in on the reading, too. When you experience the joy of reading together, a love of books becomes a lifetime pursuit for the entire family.

On the Town

Bookstore Days

Make it a ritual to introduce your youngster to new books every Saturday morning. Go to the bookstore or library, choose a few new titles, and let the child pick out some books of his or her own.

Library Card

Give your little one his or her very first library card. The library card is a right of passage. It means your child is no longer a toddler—he or she is big enough to have a card of his or her own. With a library card, your little one has a world of books at his or her fingertips. How exciting it is to be able to check out any book in the whole library!

Story Hour

Get on your library's mailing list to keep up with the different readings and activities. This is a great way to introduce kids to new books—and a group setting.

Neighborhood Jaunt

Carpool with other families to library story hours, or take turns hosting your own. Encourage your child to lend or trade books with friends, and recruit the neighborhood kids to stage a scene from a favorite book. The reading opportunities are endless.

Volunteer to Read

Visit schools, nursing homes, or hospitals and share your favorite tales. When your child sees how important reading is to you, he or she will want to make it a habit.

Public Performances

Keep abreast of plays, performances, poetry readings, and other programs in your community. Your child will enjoy them as much as you will.

Supermarket Fun

As you walk up and down the aisles of the supermarket, point to simple words and pictures on cans and boxes, such as MILK, CORN, RICE, and BEANS. Show your child that the words and pictures mean the same thing.

Take Note!

When making a special visit to a new part of town, pretend you will be writing a book about the experience. Teach your child to take mental notes of the interesting things you see together and explain how important it is to pay special attention to details. Jot down your child's observations, and let him or her sketch a scene for the book.

On the Town

In the Car

Books on Tape

Before you buckle up, pop in a book on tape. Children love listening to their favorite stories over and over again, so keep a couple of tapes in the car, especially for long rides.

Bag Those Books

The minutes will fly by once your little one gets into a good book. Keep a bag of books tucked away in the car. If the child can't read the words, he or she can at least read the pictures!

Share a Story

On quick car trips, retell a story to your child, then let your youngster retell another. Your child's version may be better than the original.

A Book for the Road

Ask carpoolers to bring along their favorite books. A carload of happy, reading children is much better than a noisy pack of restless youngsters.

"And Then . . ."

This is a great activity for carpoolers! State the first line of the story, then have each passenger add another sentence. The story can go on and on until you reach your destination.

Chapter 3

Writing

Give children the time, materials, and encouragement they need, and their love for writing will blossom.

When your little one is old enough to hold a writing utensil (without putting it in his or her mouth), give your child a crayon and a blank piece of paper. Let the youngster make squiggles and lines to his or her heart's content. Once he or she becomes proficient with crayons, move on to washable markers, watercolors, and pens (pencils are too dangerous at this point). Your youngster will be able to "draw" before he or she can form letters and words, so encourage pictures and markings whenever you can. The writing will follow soon enough.

Letters

Young children may not have the motor skills to draw letters, but they can learn to recognize them in print. Help your child learn one letter at a time, and before you know it, your little one will have conquered the entire alphabet.

At Home

Magnetic Letters

Let your child play with magnetic letters to become familiar with their different shapes. When he or she begins to show an interest, tell the child the names of the letters. Explain that letters can be strung together to spell out words, then spell out your little one's name.

Pictures and Words

Open up a book and help your child connect the printed words with the pictures. This is a new concept for little ones, so go slowly.

The ABCs

Give your child a copy of the ABCs. But remember, at this point, you are only trying to help your child understand what letters are. It isn't important to teach the entire alphabet just yet.

At Home

Letter Hunt

Once your child can point out letters, walk through the house and see how many objects you can find that have letters on them. Look on toys, cereal boxes, clothing tags, toothbrushes, and kitchen appliances. (Your child might confuse letters with numbers at this point, but don't worry—he or she will learn the difference.)

Alphabet Soup

Share a nice warm bowl of alphabet soup. With each spoonful, identify a letter by name and see if your child can find another just like it. Children can practice with dry alphabet-shaped cereal or pasta, too.

While You Wait

Give your child a place mat with letters on it. While your little one waits for Mom or Dad to dish out the food, the child can practice identifying letters or tracing them with his or her finger.

Letter Puzzles

Buy durable foam letter puzzles, and let your child spread the alphabet clear across the living room!

At Home

Toothpick Alphabet

Have your little one make letters out of tooth-picks or Popsicle sticks. The letters S and O can be quite a challenge for children, but problem solving is an important part of learning.

Word for Word

Using a black marker, write simple words on a set of cards. Next, copy these words onto another set of cards so you have two identical sets. Mix the cards together and have your child find the matching pairs.

Body Letters

When kids get bored, challenge them to form letters with their bodies! L and T are easy, but S and Q will bring squeals of laughter from the little ones. This is a great rainy-day activity when you have a bored group of kids on your hands.

Letters on the Wall

Make letters out of beans, beads, or dry macaroni and glue them on paper for a unique wall hanging. (This is a great activity on a rainy day!)

At Home

Liquid Alphabet

Using a paintbrush and a bucket of water, write a letter on the sidewalk and have your child guess the letter before it dries and disappears. This can be especially challenging on a windy day.

Letter Bingo

Make a few game cards, writing down letters that your child will recognize (and a few that he or she won't). Call out random letters and have your child cover them with buttons or Cheerios.

Alphabet Challenge

Give your child a magazine and challenge him or her to circle one of every letter of the alphabet. When time is short, see if your youngster can find only the letters that make up his or her name.

Mail Delivery

Go with your child to get the mail from the mailbox. See if he or she can recognize the first letter of the first name on each envelope. With a little practice, your little one will be able to deliver most of the mail to the correct recipients.

At Home

Alphabet Egg Carton

Write a different letter on the bottom of each section of an empty egg carton. Put a penny in it, close it, shake it, and open it again. What letter did the penny land on?

Letter of the Week

Cut out magazine pictures that begin with the letter A, look for the letter on billboards, and show your child how to write it on paper. Review the letter over and over again, and, by the end of the week, your child will know it inside and out.

Turn Letters into Art!

Gather glue, glitter, buttons, paper, fabric scraps, and anything else you can think of. Have your child use these materials to make his or her letter of the week.

Walking Letters

It seems like everybody wears letters these days! Next time you walk through town, look for letters on tee shirts, hats, shoes, and jackets.

Supermarket Search

As you linger in the cereal aisle, have your little one search for an S while you decide which brand to buy.

Letters at the Library

Look for books that pay special attention to your letter of the week, and point this letter out as you read aloud to your youngster.

Letters on the Town

Look for the letter T on signs around town. Your child will be so tuned into the letter that he or she will spot it way before you do.

Food Fun

When kids go out to eat, encourage them to make letters out of French fries, carrots, pretzel sticks, and any other food worth dawdling over. Have your child eat the letters as he or she goes.

On the Town

In the Car

What's in a Name?

Give your child each letter of his or her name on separate index cards and let him or her practice putting them in order on the way to and from the supermarket. Call out one letter at a time, and give your youngster plenty of time to find the right card.

Letters on the Road

Have your youngster watch for letters on road signs, store fronts, and license plates. Your child can shout them out as you drive by!

Mix and Match

Give your child a magnetic or paper alphabet, along with simple three-letter words written on index cards. Ask the child to match the alphabet letters to the letters on the cards.

The ABC Song

Sing the ABC song as you wind down the road. Kids love to sing, and your child can never hear this song too often.

License Plate Letters

Write your child's name on a piece of paper, then see if the youngster can find each letter of his or her name in the license plates that go by.

Letters and Sound Recognition

Once children become familiar with the concept of letters, parents can help identify the sounds that go with them. For instance, when your youngster looks at the letter K, he or she needs to know that K has a k-k-k sound. Make the sound for your child and suggest several words that begin with this sound. The relationship between the letter and its sound will help the child later when he or she learns to read.

At Home

Sight and Sound

Make a set of flashcards containing all the letters of the alphabet. For each card, say the letter's sound and have the child repeat it. Then ask the child to think of words that might start with that letter.

Whether it takes a few days or a few weeks, don't move on until the youngster has mastered the letter at hand. Be sure to periodically review the letters he or she has learned. When your little one becomes more advanced, the child can try putting the flashcards in alphabetical order.

At Home

An ABC Book

While making the t-t-t sound, help your child identify the letter T. Next, look for magazine pictures that start with this sound, cut them out, and glue them to blank pages. Let your child dictate a story to go with the pictures while you write down his or her words. Finally, add construction paper for the cover and tie all the pages together with colorful yarn. Make a book for each sound, or make one big book full of several different sounds.

Sounds Like . . .

Put a big D on your little one's doll, dinosaur, dress, desk, drawers, dresser, and anything else that begins with that letter. Label objects that begin with a different letter every week.

Animal Alphabet Book

Pick a subject and let your child create a page for each letter. For animals, start with ant, bear, cat, dog, elephant, fox, goat, horse—and don't forget the illustrations!

At Home

The Guessing Game

Ask your child to guess what letter you're thinking of. Feel free to give hints: "My letter is the first letter of one of your friends' names," or "You have a board game that begins with this letter."

Letter Blocks

Children love to play with blocks, so buy some letter blocks for your little one. Have the child pick a letter, make its sound, then build something that begins with that sound.

Room Full of Letters

"How many objects in this room start with the letter B?" List the objects on a chalkboard or piece of paper, so your child can copy them in an alphabet book later on.

What's for Supper?

Let your child guess what's for supper. "It starts with t-t-t. It's a type of bird, and I bake it in the oven. What is it?"

At Home

Pictures to Words

Make two sets of index cards, one with words, the other with corresponding pictures. Have your child sound out the words and match them to the illustrations.

Alphabet Cassette

Tape-record all the alphabet sounds, pausing after each one. As your child plays back the cassette, he or she can shout out the correct letter during the pause: a-a-a (pause—"A!"), b-b-b (pause—"B!"), and so forth. With an alphabet tape, your child can practice sound recognition anytime he or she wants to.

On the Town

Take a Walk

Go for a nice, long walk and see how many objects your child can identify that begin with the the s-s-s sound. "Sky, sun, stick, sand, stone, squirrel, sparrow, spider . . ." the list could go on and on!

The Waiting Game

Hunt for letters at the checkout line or doctor's office. Pick a sound and see how many objects your child can find that start with that sound. An unpleasant wait won't seem so bad with the ABCs to pass the time.

Letter Collection

If P is the letter of the week, take a walk and look for objects that start with the p-p-p sound. Bring home pinecones, pebbles, petunias, and pansies for your child to use in an art project later.

B Is for "Bowling Alley"

Visit someplace that begins with your letter of the week. Go to the art museum, bowling alley, candy store, dinosaur exhibit, and any other location that is alphabetically correct. Be creative!

On the Town

Sweet Rewards

After a week of hard learning, reward your youngster with a trip to the local dollar store. Let your child buy one or two small items that begin with the letter of the week.

Alphabet in a Bag

On your next trip to the doctor's office, bring a bag filled with several small objects. Ask your little one to select an object from the bag and say its name. The child must then try to determine what letter the object starts with.

Smile for the Camera

Help your child photograph objects around town that begin with a particular letter. When the photos come back, your child can put them in a special ABC book.

Letters in the Sky

Lay on your back on a beautiful summer day and see if you and your youngster can find clouds that resemble letters. If the clouds resemble objects, what does the name of each object start with?

Let's Go to Sharon's House!

Write or visit a friend whose name begins with the letter of the week. Have your child pick out a small gift to bring along, but make sure it begins with the right letter!

In the Car

Sound Off!

Take turns thinking of words that begin with the t-t-t sound. For a challenge, think of words that have something to do with cars, like traffic, truck, tire, turn, and taxi.

I Spy

As you travel along, look for objects that begin with a certain sound. "I spy a boat, a boy, a brick wall, and a baby!" Try playing this game in alphabetical order: "I spy an alley, a bicycle, a car . . ." and so forth.

License Plate Fun

Make the s-s-s sound and have your child find the matching letter on a license plate. See if you can go through the whole alphabet before you reach your destination.

Do You Know Any Xs?

Brainstorm the names of all the people you know. What sounds do they begin with? On long car trips, try this game in alphabetical order.

Alternate Alliterations

What big words for little kids! Don't bother defining them—just jump right in. For T, try "Two tiny toads tickle Todd."

Writing the Alphabet

"Look what I wrote!" your child says proudly, handing you a paper full of scribbly lines. At first, you fail to see anything that even resembles a letter. On closer inspection, however, you realize that there are signs of actual writing on the paper.

This is the first indication that your child is interested in forming letters to create words. If you ask your youngster to read the words to you, he or she will proudly spout off an entire sentence. The child *did* write something on the paper, just not in a language that grown-ups can understand.

Parents, teachers, and researchers all have different opinions about whether to start children with uppercase or lowercase letters, or both at the same time. Before you begin teaching your child to write, you may want to contact his or her future teacher to see how letters are taught in your school district. Consider, too, that some teachers are strict about letter formation, so ask for advice on this as well. If your youngster learns to make letters correctly, he or she won't have to change handwriting habits when school starts.

When your little one is ready to learn how to write, have the child decide which hand to use. Then, position the writing utensil correctly in the child's hand, making sure his or her fingers are about an inch from the point. Let your son or daughter practice making scribbles and lines before you begin to teach letter formation.

At Home

Texture

Make a felt or sandpaper alphabet and mount the letters on light cardboard. Each time you introduce a new letter, have your child trace it with his or her finger to get an idea of how the letter is written.

Yummy Messy Letters

Pour dry Jell-O onto a tray, write a letter on a piece of paper, then let your child trace that letter in the Jell-O. Flour and powdered sugar work, too, and they make enough of a mess to keep kids interested. For even more fun (and more mess), try tracing letters in whipped cream.

Ooey Gooey Letters

Encourage finger painters to add letters to their latest masterpiece. Or better yet, drop a few tablespoons of chocolate pudding onto waxed paper. Let children trace letters in the chocolate—if they get the letters right, they can lick their fingers!

Tracing

Let your child experiment with tracing paper—freehand letter formation will come later.

At Home

Cookie Cutter Letters

Letter-shaped cookie cutters make more than just cookies! Children can munch away on their ABCs while tracing the cutters on paper.

Dot to Dot

Draw dots to form the pattern of a letter. Once your child can confidently connect the dots, see if he or she can write the letter independently!

Portable Chalkboards

A chalkboard is much more appealing than simple paper and pen, so tote a little chalkboard everywhere you go. When you write a letter on the board, your child can copy it right then and there.

Ready? Set? Go!

Give your child sixty seconds to draw all the letters that he or she can think of. Different children require different time limits, of course.

Sidewalk Silliness

Bring out a bucket of sidewalk chalk! Write letters on the driveway or sidewalk, and have your child copy them in another color. Kids can do this for hours.

At Home

Activity Books

There are plenty of books available to help children practice uppercase and lowercase letters. But don't "assign" pages—you don't want to discourage little ones at such an early age. Simply let children work at their own pace. If they're not interested, don't force it.

Glitter and Glue

Use glue to write letters on construction paper. Cover the glue with glitter or ice cream sprinkles, let it dry, and post the masterpiece on the refrigerator door!

Fabric Paint

Help kids write their name on hats, sweatshirts, and shoes with fabric paint from your local craft store. Children will proudly wear their writing wherever they go.

Student or Teacher?

Let your child be the teacher every now and then, so he or she can show *you* how to write a letter. This is the perfect opportunity to check your child's progress.

At Home

Copycats

Once children can copy letters, invite them to copy words. Write simple words on paper and let your child copy the series of letters. Imagine the accomplishment little ones feel when they realize they have written their very first word!

Book of Letters

Help your child make a book of letters to display his or her hard work. Keep writing samples along the way, so your child can see his or her progress.

One Letter at a Time

Children are thrilled to see their name in print, and learning to write it themselves is a magnificent accomplishment. Write your child's name on his or her books, coats, jackets, art projects—everything he or she owns. Then, help your child practice writing his or her name, one letter at a time. This may take several days, or even a few weeks, but it will be well worth it. Once your little one can write his or her name, encourage the child to write it on every project he or she completes. Remember, practice makes perfect!

Games Galore

Visit the library or bookstore for books and games that will help your child learn to write. You'll be surprised at how much is out there!

Checkout Line

While waiting in line at the supermarket or library, use your finger to trace a letter on your child's back, then see if he or she can guess what it is. It takes some concentration, but your little one will get the hang of it. Let the child trace letters on your back, too, so you can be the guesser!

Rainy-Day Fun

Take a long walk after a hard rain, find a stick, and write letters in the mud. Your little one will be thrilled to play in the mud, dirt, sand, or any other messy place.

Snowprints

Go for a walk on a winter day, call out the letters of your little one's name, and ask the child to stomp each letter in the snow. Afterward, have your child step back to view the masterpiece.

On the Town

In the Car

Chalkboard for the Road

Keep a small chalkboard in the car. Long rides won't seem so bad if your little one can pass the time with his or her ABCs.

Calling All Cars

Call out the letters you see on license plates and have your child write them down. When you arrive at your destination, praise your youngster for his or her fine penmanship.

Alphabet in the Window

Breathe on the window one frosty morning and write letters in the steam. Call out different letters and let your little one trace them with one finger.

The Thrill of Writing

Kids have a knack for wanting to do things they aren't able to do yet. They see their parents writing out checks, preparing grocery lists, and jotting off letters. Writing intrigues them, and they want to do it, too.

Once your child is ready to write independently, don't let the interest slip away. Find activities that will keep the excitement alive.

At Home

Write about It

Next time you come home from a family outing, have your child write a story about it. Write down his or her words, and resist the urge to correct grammatical errors. After all, would you want someone to change *your* story?

Once you've got the story down on paper, read it over to see if the child would like to make any changes. Invite the youngster to draw pictures to accompany the writing.

Daily Journal

Just before bedtime, jot down a few sentences—in your child's own words—about something interesting that happened that day. Before you know it, your son or daughter will be keeping the journal on his or her own.

At Home

Cordial Correspondence

Buy some children's stationery and jot down your youngster's words as he or she dictates birthday cards, thank-you cards, and letters to friends and family. Let your son or daughter write his or her own name, if the child is able.

Magical Writing Machines

Introduce your child to computers, typewriters, and word processors. Children are intrigued with these technological wonders, so let your child hunt and peck—under your supervision, of course. You might even buy a "children's computer" for hours of writing enjoyment.

Family Newsletter

Start a family newsletter. Put your child in charge of a section, or let the youngster help with the entire project! Include tidbits about the children's soccer tournament, the success of your flower garden, or your last family vacation. Let your child decorate the newsletter and assist with its distribution.

Book List

Ask your child to trace or copy the titles he or she checks out from the library. Save these titles—soon your child will have a complete list of all the books he or she read that year. What an accomplishment!

Don't Forget the Crayons

When you go out to eat, bring paper and crayons along. Let your child trace words from the menu or make up stories about the food he or she has ordered.

Big Blank Book

Before you leave on your family vacation, give your child a journal to bring along. Help your child keep a diary of his or her experiences throughout the trip. By the time you get back home, the child will have a wonderful book of memories.

On the Town

On the Town

Postcards

Let your child pick out cards to send to friends and relatives. You can write the words while your child dictates. (This is a great opportunity to introduce the concepts of stamps and addresses, too.)

Hotel Stationery

At every hotel, make a point of using the hotel stationery to write to friends and family. Your child might even use this stationery as a sort of journal, writing letters to himself or herself and mailing them home. When the little one gets back from vacation, he or she will have special letters waiting in the mailbox.

Personal Touch

Let your child pick out his or her very own stationery at the card shop. Better yet, make your own stationery out of multicolored paper.

Capture the Moment

When you get the photographs back from your family vacation, have your child dictate the captions. Your youngster's words will be memorialized in the photo album for years to come.

In the Car

The Secret Word

Choose one child in your car pool to sound out a simple word on paper, then have him or her drop hints to the other passengers to see if they can guess the word. "It's an animal and Alexander has one at home." When the kids guess "cat," see if they can figure out how to spell it!

Take a Left

Ask your child to note your directions as you drive. "On the way to Faye's house, we pull out of the driveway, take a left, and drive all the way to the end of the street. Then we take a right and keep driving until we come to the brown building."

The "directions" are likely to look like pictures and squiggles at first, but as your little one becomes more proficient with letters (and learns to distinguish left from right), he or she will eventually begin to write with words.

In the Car

Tiny Tour Guides

Give your child a tape recorder so he or she can dictate into the microphone as you drive. Let the youngster talk about where you are going, how you are getting there, and all the interesting things you see along the way.

Weather Journal

Have your youngster draw the weather every day. If he or she is able, let the child write a letter that describes the picture he or she has drawn. C is for cloudy, S is for sun or snow, and so forth. Be sure to have your child guess what the weather will be like tomorrow, too. Will it be sunny, rainy, windy, or cloudy? Check if the forecast was accurate. Soon, your child will be able to write whole words alongside his or her pictures!

Chapter 4

Numbers, Shapes, and Colors

Many children find math to be their favorite subject; others develop math anxiety, making an already difficult subject seem even more frustrating. Make the introduction to numbers a pleasant and engaging experience. Begin with counting. In no time at all, your youngster will be counting everything in sight, from blocks to candy to people.

Once your little one learns to count, move on to writing and number recognition, then try harder concepts like money, measurement, and how to tell time. Throw in some shapes and colors, and your child will have a great head start when he or she gets to school.

Counting

Grown-ups count everything, from the errands we run to the minutes it takes to prepare a meal. Counting seems so basic that we tend to forget how difficult it can be for children. As with most math activities, kids need to be introduced to counting in stages, then given many, many opportunities to practice. Let your child conquer 1 through 5 before working on 6 through 10. Introduce one or two new numbers at a time, and praise your child's progress.

At Home

Matching Buttons

Learning to match quantities is the first step on the road to counting. Place three buttons in a row, then ask your child to place the same number of buttons across from yours. Once your youngster masters buttons, move on to blocks of different shapes, sizes, and colors. Place a few blocks in a row and challenge your child to match the pattern, block by block.

More or Less

Lay out two rows of buttons—a row of three and a row of four. Ask your child to place the exact same number of buttons across from each row. Then ask which group has more. Once your child understands the concept of "more," ask which row has "less." It will take some practice, but your child will soon understand the difference.

Sort and Count

Dump a handful of beads on the table and ask your child to group them according to color, then according to size and shape. The ability to group objects is another prerequisite for counting.

Count Everything

Before your child can even pronounce the numbers, show him or her what the numbers mean. Begin by counting everything—and I mean everything—out loud. Count steps when you go up the stairs. When you come back down, count them again. When you read a book together, count the people on the pages or the animals in the barn. Before long, your child will be counting right around with you. Try counting:

- People in your family

- Foods on the plate

- Items in the shopping cart

- Baseball cards

- Crayons

- Cans in the cupboard

- The number of seconds between lightning and thunder

- Snowflakes that land on your hand

- Stars

- Birds at the feeder

At Home

Board Games

Many board games require children to count, although you may have to help them along until they can move the pieces and count on their own.

Snack Time

When your child asks for candy, say, "You may have three pieces." Your little one will learn to count to three in no time at all!

Chores

Tell your little one that if he or she can pick up six blocks, you'll pick up the rest.

Suppertime Assistance

Kids can count while setting the table: "Tommi Ann, we need four spoons, four forks, four knives, and four napkins—one for each of us."

Cooking, too, can teach your child about the need for numbers and counting. "Can you count out five hamburger buns?" "We need one teaspoon of salt. What would our cake taste like if we put in five teaspoons of salt instead?" Your child will be so pleased to help that math will seem like an adventure!

On the Town

Family Vacation

When you're on vacation, count skyscrapers, palm trees, new foods, the people you meet, and the hours at the beach. Cross off the days you've been there and count how many days you have left. Have your youngster start a seashell or postcard collection, then count the shells or cards when you get back home. Take every opportunity to count, count, count!

Picture Book Counting

Count on picture books to help build those number skills! "Let's count the balls on this page." "How many cows does the farmer have to milk?" Take your child to the bookstore and peruse the aisles for counting books.

A Walk in the Woods

Go on a nature walk. Look for pinecones or maple leaves and count the squirrels, butterflies, and wildflowers. Not only will your child practice counting, he or she might discover a life-long love of the outdoors.

Exercise Those Number Skills!

How many times can your child jump rope without missing? How many times can he or she hit the baseball? Kids fill their days with sports and recreation—the trick is to think how each activity might give them a chance to practice counting.

On the Town

Picnic Counting

Invite the neighborhood kids on a picnic. Count the people who come, the foods you eat, the bugs that visit—let the children count anything they can see.

Sing Along

Jazz up those numbers with counting songs! Kids love to sing, and parents should take advantage of it. "One, Two, Buckle My Shoe," "This Old Man," and "1, 2, 3, 4, 5, I Caught a Fish Alive" are great counting practice. Visit your local library or music store to find tapes and CDs especially for children. If you and your child are creative types, try making up new words to go with old tunes!

Supermarket Helpers

If you need one box of cereal and three green apples, have your little one count them out.

Fall Fun

As soon as the leaves start to change, take a long walk and count the leaves you see on the ground. Bring home the prettiest leaves, separate them by color, and count the leaves in each group. Are there more red, yellow, or brown leaves this year?

In the Car

Red Car, Blue Car

Have carpoolers count all the red cars that drive by. See who can find the most, and help the children keep score. Switch colors on the ride home.

It's a Dog's World

Challenge everyone in the car to count every dog they see. On the way back home, pick a less common animal and see who can spot it first.

Counting Cows

If you live in the country, count cows or farms on the way to the market. If you live in the city, count traffic lights or police officers.

Keep Counting

On a rainy day, have your youngster count the passengers, windows, and radio knobs in the car. Count stop signs, cars that drive by, and anything else that might keep a bored child occupied until you reach your destination.

Reading and Writing Numbers

Once your child learns to count, it's time to move on to reading and writing numbers. Work on one number at a time, and don't move on until the child has mastered that number.

Most children find the number 1 easiest to start with. Of course, if your child wants to start with the number 4 because he or she is four years old, by all means, start with 4. Do whatever it takes to make learning as easy and exciting as possible.

At Home

Paper and Penny

Write the numbers 1 through 10 on different pieces of paper. Ask the child to place a corresponding number of pennies on each. If your little one is more advanced, have the child put the cards in numerical order.

Dominoes

Make a set of paper dominoes with a numeral on one half and a corresponding number of dots on the other. Cut the dominoes in half and have the child match the numerals to the dots.

At Home

Numbers in a Flash

Make two identical sets of number flashcards, mix them up in a large envelope, and have your child match the pairs.

Caterpillar Puzzle

Cut out seven circles. On one circle, draw a face resembling that of a caterpillar. On another, draw a spike to resemble a tail. Number the remaining circles 1 through 5. Have your child put the caterpillar together by placing the head and tail in the front and back, with the numbers 1 through 5 ordered between them. Other simple puzzles might be a train, wiener dog, snowman, or ice cream cone.

The Sunday Paper

Spend a lazy Sunday morning perusing the newspaper. Your child can highlight numbers with a marker, or better yet, cut them out and glue them on paper to make a number collage.

Macaroni Numbers

Write a large number on a piece of construction paper and have your child glue uncooked macaroni on top. If you're short on pasta, try toothpicks or dry cereal instead.

At Home

Number Bingo

Make simple bingo cards displaying numbers familiar to your child. Use pennies for markers. Announce each number, and see if your child can find it on the card. You may need to help your youngster at first, but the child will soon learn to find the numbers independently. Make new bingo cards as your child learns new numbers.

Bird Watching

Birds fly away so quickly! Instead of writing down a number each time a bird appears, it may be faster to tally the birds as they come. Teach your child how to draw vertical lines side by side, one for each bird. When he or she gets to the number five, the child can draw a horizontal line through the four vertical lines. Count all the lines at the end, and write the total in numerals.

Height Chart

Post a height chart in your child's room and record your little one's growth every few months. Your youngster will be thrilled to know that he or she is getting bigger all the time. More importantly, the child will see that all these numbers really mean something.

At Home

Numbers on the Fridge

Buy a package of magnetic numbers to keep on the refrigerator door. Your child will gravitate toward these numbers the next time he or she lingers in the kitchen looking for food or waiting for you to get off the phone.

A Roll of the Dice

Once your child can count to six, point out that each side of a dice has dots representing a different number. Roll the dice several times and take turns counting the dots. Before you know it, your youngster will have mastered a whole new skill!

Pass the Remote

Youngsters are intrigued with remotes from the moment they see them click on the TV. Supervise your child as he or she changes channels with the remote control. Before long, your child will be a pro at numbers (especially the ones that turn on his or her favorite shows).

Calendars from Years Gone By

Never throw out an old calendar—your youngster can practice copying numbers in the little squares.

At Home

Number 1

When children practice writing a number, they often need to have a copy of the number nearby. You may want to keep a set of number flashcards or a number line on hand.

Draw the number 1 five times, then have your child trace over the numbers with a colored pencil or marker. Once your little one understands how a number is formed, he or she can try drawing it independently. Praise the youngster's efforts—he or she will get much better with practice and encouragement.

A Number Book

Have your child cut out one animal from a magazine, glue it to a piece of construction paper, and draw the number 1 at the bottom of the page. Cut out two animals for the next page, three for the next, and so forth until your youngster has ten full pages of numbers! Add new pages as the child learns new numbers, and tie them together with colorful yarn.

Basic Workbooks

Some children thrive with workbooks, others find them boring. Have your child try one and see how it goes. Resist the urge to sit your child down and demand three pages now and three pages after supper. Math should be fun, not forced!

At Home

Get Ready to Write!

When writing numbers, don't limit your child to pens and pencils—use vibrant colors and sticky, messy substances.

- Spray a plastic picnic table with shaving cream and let your child write numbers in the foam.

- Trace numbers in the sand with Popsicle sticks.

- Go outside after a hard rain, find a stick, and write numbers in the mud.

- Sidewalk chalk is fun in the summer.

- White chalk looks great on black construction paper.

- Finger paints are fun, too. Paint swirls and twirls with numbers in between.

- If you have a group of children on a rainy day, give them a number and see if they can form that number with their bodies. The numbers 1 and 7 are simple; the fun begins with 3 and 8!

- Washable markers are fun to use, and they won't stain clothes, hands, or kitchen tables.

- Practice bold, beautiful numbers with water colors and paint brushes.

On the Town

Calculators on the Go

Bring a calculator to the supermarket and let your child punch in or add up the prices of food items as you go. This way, your little one can "help" keep track of the costs.

Rainy-Day Adventure

After a hard rain, take a walk through the neighborhood, find a big stick, and make numbers in the mud.

Hit the Beach

Build sandcastles together and practice writing numbers in the wet sand.

In the Car

Calculator Time

Call out numbers and have your child punch them in on the calculator. Once your little one masters this little game, addition and subtraction won't be far behind. When you think your youngster is ready, introduce the plus, minus, and equal signs. Who says little kids are too young to do math?

Name That Number

Have your child point to number signs as you drive by. Look for speed limits, route numbers, and other signs along the way.

Write and Ride

Keep a chalkboard, writing board, or pen and paper in the car. When a car ride becomes unbearable, the child can practice his or her numbers to pass the time.

Pick a Number

Pick a number, then have your child try to find it on the road. Look at road signs, store fronts, billboards, license plates—any number is fair game, as long as it's outside the car.

Street Numbers

Even if you know exactly where you're going, have your child look for the address as you come close to your destination. Some addresses have several numbers, so give your little one lots of help as you go.

Measurement

Whether they know it or not, little kids have already begun to measure the world around them. They notice if an older sibling gets a bigger slice of cake for dessert. On the playground, they strive to swing higher and higher. At supper, they want more cookies and less broccoli.

When teaching different concepts of measurement, start with simple lessons and build upon your child's experiences.

At Home

Bigger and Smaller

When putting away the groceries, place a can of soda and a box of cereal in front of your child, then ask which is larger. Do this several times with different objects to reinforce the concept. Next, place a tomato beside a loaf of bread and ask which is smaller. Give your child plenty of practice to let these concepts sink in.

Heavier and Lighter

Give your child two objects of very different weights, such as a book and a piece of paper. Ask the youngster which is heavier. (Children often think that bigger objects automatically weigh more, so this activity might be even more challenging than the last.) After your child has had some practice with "heavier," introduce the word "lighter."

Longer and Shorter

Have your child cut two pieces of string. Which is longer? Which is shorter? Cut a third piece of string and explain, "This one is long, this one is longer, this one is longest." Once these ideas sink in, have the youngster cut some new string and try it again.

Taller and Shorter

Who is the tallest person in your family? Who is the shortest? Look for tall people and short people at the library, on the street, and in magazines. Once your child understands the difference, introduce tall, taller, and tallest, then short, shorter, and shortest. Don't forget to mention that some people will be the same height.

Measuring Tools

Keep a variety of measuring utensils nearby, including rulers, yardsticks, height charts, bathroom scales, and measuring cups. If you leave these in your child's play or work area, he or she may be intrigued enough to use them.

Measurement Words

Use measurement words in everyday conversation with your child. "Let's see who can throw the ball the farthest." "You are growing so tall that these pants don't fit you anymore!" Hearing the terms over and over again will help reinforce these difficult concepts.

At Home

Area

"How many dominoes would it take to fill this paper?" This question prompts children to make a guess about the area of an object. Understanding what "area" means is not important at this age, but a basic introduction will help when your youngster starts to learn about it in school.

Fractions

"I'm going to eat an apple. Would you like half?" Introduce basic fractions when cutting a pizza, dividing up chores, or playing with toys.

Liquids

Kids have a grand time with measuring cups in the bathtub! Pouring water from one cup to another teaches them a little about liquid capacity, and it makes bath time less of a battle for parents.

Solids

Let children play with measuring cups in the sandbox. How many scoops of sand will it take to fill a bucket? Kids will quickly become absorbed in scooping and measuring on their own.

Measuring Ingredients

Whenever you cook or bake, let your child lend a hand. How many cans of water does it take to make lemonade? How many teaspoons of salt should we put in the cookie batter? With each and every project, your child will learn something new about measuring.

Make Your Own Measurement

"Our porch is twenty-five footsteps long." "How many paper clips long is this paper?" See who can come up with the wackiest measurement.

On the Town

Compare and Contrast

Measure food items at the supermarket. Compare cereal box sizes, guess how many cases of soda will fit under the cart, and see who can find the biggest apple. Be creative, and let your child choose items to measure, too.

The Limitless Library

While looking for books about measurement, search out the highest shelves, the heaviest books, and the shortest line at the checkout counter.

Kiddie Contest

Recruit children on the playground and hold a contest to see who can jump the highest, run the farthest, and yell the loudest. Give everyone a chance to win: Who can hold their breath the longest? Who can crouch the lowest?

Distance in Feet—A Kid's Feet!

Have your little one walk heel to toe from the car to the library. How many steps did it take?

In the Car

The Miles Fly By

Show your child exactly how long a mile is. Point out road signs that tell you how many miles there are to your destination, and keep track of the miles as you travel from one place to another.

Timing the Traffic Lights

Count how many seconds it takes to drive from one traffic light to the next. Your child will learn a whole new way to measure distance!

Measurement Games

"Which is bigger, an elephant or a dog?" "Whose house is farther away, Grandma's or Uncle John's?" Make the questions harder and harder, and let your child make up questions, too.

Stoplights

Count the stoplights on the way to daycare, the supermarket, and the mall. How many stoplights is it to Allison's house? To the library?

Money

Children come in contact with coins at an early age and, when they find out they can trade these little shiny circles for toys and candy, they want to know more. When teaching children about money, it's best to start with simple money facts and build on what they already know.

At Home

What Is Money?

Use simple terms to explain what money is: The round circles are coins and the paper rectangles are bills. Moms and Dads can get these pieces of money for the work they do. We can take this money to the market and trade it for food, clothing, and other things we need.

Coins

Let children play with coins—it's an excellent opportunity to introduce them to the different sizes, colors, and designs. But use caution: Children can choke if they put coins in their mouth. Never allow youngsters to play with money without your supervision.

Play Money

Invest in a package of durable play money, and have your youngster match the play money with real money.

At Home

A Penny for Your Thoughts

Tell the child that a penny is worth one cent. A single penny won't buy much—maybe a small gumball or one piece of candy—but put five pennies in a row, and you can exchange them for a nickel. A nickel equals five cents. With five cents, you can buy a bigger gumball or five pieces of candy!

Next, place two nickels in a row, then exchange them for a dime. A dime might buy a lollipop. Tell your child that ten cents can be made with ten pennies, two nickels, or a dime.

It may take days or weeks to help a child understand the values of coins. Go slowly, and try not to let your child get too frustrated.

Hidden Coins

Hide a coin in your hand and ask your child to guess what it is. When you open your hand, have the child name the coin and see if his or her guess was correct. With constant practice, your child will learn the names of the coins as well as their values.

Coins can be difficult for children to identify. Kids might memorize the differences, but it takes a great deal of practice to actually *understand* them. Games that repeat the names and values over and over again will help.

At Home

Money of Their Own

What better way to help your little one understand the concept of money than to give the child some money of his or her own? Many parents give their children a weekly allowance to encourage saving. Other parents prefer to pay their children to do chores—ten cents for helping with the dishes, fifteen cents for making the bed. Still others simply give their children a little money now and then—the leftover change from the supermarket, any stray coins the kids find while tidying the house, or money from the bottom of a purse or desk drawer.

Business Experience

Set up a lemonade stand or hold a yard sale. A little "business experience" will give your child a chance to earn some money on his or her own.

Off to the "Market"

Set out a calculator, a box of play money, and some cans of food from the kitchen cupboard. Take turns playing the customer—this is an excellent opportunity for your child to watch how money works!

The Money Jar

If your family is saving for a vacation or a new television, let your child contribute to the savings. Open the jar every now and then and count the money to see how much you still need.

At Home

Math for "Big Kids"

Teach your child to add dollars on a calculator the way big kids do. Start with simple word problems: "Livia is buying a sweater for $2 and a shirt for $3. How much will it cost her? What is 2 plus 3?"

Coupon Clipping

Your child can master dollars and cents by helping you cut coupons for the supermarket. Let the child keep the money saved in exchange for his or her scissor work. Better yet, start a savings jar and spend the coupon money on something special for both of you.

Flip That Flashcard!

Tape coins on flashcards and write their values on the back. While Mom and Dad are busy doing grown-up chores, the child can learn about money on his or her own.

Coin Rubbing

Place a coin under thin paper and rub gently over it with a pencil. Ta-da! An image of the coin appears like magic. Kids love this trick, and it helps reinforce coin recognition.

On the Town

Savings Account

Open a savings account and urge your child to save at least $20 by the end of the year. Speculate on what he or she might do with the money. Is the child saving for a toy? For spending money to use on vacation? Build excitement about savings now, and your child will exercise financial responsibility throughout his or her lifetime.

Spending Money

Take your little one to the market and let the child spend some money by himself or herself. Direct experience is always the best way to learn.

The Price Is Right

At the supermarket, have your little one read off the prices of items that you put in the shopping cart. The child will proudly practice his or her numbers while helping you "keep track of the costs."

Little Helper

Allow your child to sort and insert coins at laundromats, parking meters, and public telephones. This is a big responsibility for a little kid!

Money Exchange

Take your child to the bank to exchange bills for rolls of coins. Your child will not only see the relationship between bills and coins, he or she will have a new batch of coins to sort and count when you get home.

In the Car

Money Matters

Where does all that money go? As you drive by different buildings, have your youngster name the places where people spend money.

Coins and Their Values

On the way to the supermarket, quiz your child on the value of each coin. On the way back, call out each value and ask the child to name the coin that goes with it.

Value Games

As you drive to the store, ask your child, "Which costs more, a car or a loaf of bread?" Make the questions very easy at first, then move on to harder ones.

Telling Time

Little kids may be too young to know how a clock works, but they are certainly capable of grasping the concept of time segments. Begin with an explanation of morning, afternoon, and evening, then move on to minutes, hours, days, and weeks. Before you know it, your child will be keeping track of time everywhere you go.

At Home

Before and After

Practice these words in conversation. "Before we go to bed, we will read some books." "After we visit Aunt Gail, we will stop at the market."

TV Time

Children already know how long a commercial is—explain that this amount of time is called a minute. To reinforce this concept, let your little one watch the second hand pass a full minute on the clock.

Take Your Time

Time your youngster as he or she sings, dances, or jumps rope for a full minute, so the child can see how long a minute lasts. "See if you can go a minute without talking." "If you start picking up your toys, I will help you in one minute." "Let's see how many animals you can name in one minute. Ready? Go!"

At Home

Watch the Clock

If bedtime is 8:00, show your little one the clock every night until the child can recognize the hour whenever he or she sees it. Once the child masters 8:00, show what five or ten minutes before the hour looks like. Give the youngster ten minutes to finish playing with his or her blocks, pointing to the clock at 7:50 and again at 7:55. By the time the clock reads 8:00, ten minutes will have a little more meaning to the child.

Buy a Watch

Buy your child a watch of his or her own, but make sure it's a standard watch, not a digital one. Any child can learn to read 6:45 on a digital watch, but this has no real meaning unless he or she can tell time on a regular watch.

What Time Is It?

When your child is ready to learn how to tell time, show the youngster different clocks with different hours on them. Once he or she comprehends "o'clocks," you can move on to "half pasts," "quarters," and so forth.

On the Town

Time Your Footsteps

Take a stroll through town and have your little one take one step every second, then two steps, then three. See how far you can take this game without laughing!

Time and Temperature

Look at time and temperature signs on buildings around town. Does the time on each building match the time on your child's watch?

Time to Eat

For kids who dawdle at restaurants, challenge them to finish their entire meal in half an hour. If they manage to meet the challenge, let them take their time with dessert!

In the Car

Are We There Yet?

When kids want to know how long it will take to reach your destination, "thirty minutes" might not mean much. Instead, say, "We'll be there in the time it takes to watch *Barney*." This gives children a good idea of how long they'll be in the car.

Take Five

Challenge a group of young carpoolers to try to guess when five minutes is up. See who comes the closest. Ready? Set? Go!

How Long Will It Take?

Have your little one guess how long it will take to get to the supermarket. If he or she comes close, let the child play with a stopwatch. Your youngster can time how long you stand in the checkout line!

Days, Weeks, Months, Years

Calendars are wonderful teaching tools. They show kids that each month is divided into days, and each day has a name and a number. Once kids can locate their birthday among all those little squares, they'll be glued to the calendar, counting down the days.

At Home

Calendar Days

Hang a calendar in your child's room and circle upcoming events. This way, the child will have a visual reference nearby to reinforce his or her lessons.

Day by Day

Announce the day of the week every morning at breakfast. The child will learn the days of the week so well, he or she will soon be able to tell *you* what day it is! Once your youngster learns the days, start teaching the dates.

Birthdays

Mark your child's birthday on the calendar. Explain, "You were born on this date. See, this month has a name and each day has a number." You'll be amazed at how quickly the child learns to count down the days!

At Home

Cut It Out

Cut the months out of an old calendar, mix them up, and have your child practice putting them back in order. Once he or she learns the months, move on to the days of the week.

As Time Goes By

Have your child date his or her papers and art projects. As the years go by, your little one will have a record of his or her progress.

Homemade Calendar

Let your child copy the days from a current calendar onto twelve blank pages. Afterward, he or she can draw pictures for each month!

Growing Older Every Day

How old is your child *exactly?* Help your little one add up the years, months, weeks, days, hours, minutes, and seconds. Your child won't understand the details, but this activity is sure to grab his or her interest, and your little one will begin to see that all these time units are related.

At Home

A Book of Seasons

Time is measured in seasons, too, so watch the changes that occur outdoors. Cut out photographs of snowflakes, flowers, sunshine, and fallen leaves and place them in a seasons book. Better yet, paste actual pine needles, flowers, seashells, and colorful leaves in the book. Continue to fill these pages with the seasonal treasures you collect throughout the year.

TV Schedules

Have kids list their favorite programs, the days they are on, and the times. (This will inevitably lead to negotiations regarding the number of shows they're allowed to watch, so be prepared.)

Weekly Traditions

Take your child to the same place on the same day every week. When Thursday rolls around, say, "We're going to the park today. What day is it?" Your youngster will learn about Thursday and the length of one full week at the same time.

Seasons

As you read through library books, look closely at the pictures. Does your child see snow? Sunshine? Bare trees? Ask your youngster what time of the year it is in the pictures, then have him or her try to guess the month.

Are You Open?

Watch for business hours posted around town. Each time you arrive at a restaurant, bank, store, or post office, have your little one determine when it closes. The child will learn to look on the sign, point to the day of the week, and read off the times.

On the Town

In the Car

The Week in Review

On the way to the bank or post office, have your little one recite the days of the week, along with one thing he or she did on each day. "On Monday I did. . . . On Tuesday I. . . ."

License Plate Dates

Look for the registration dates on license plates, and keep a special eye out for plates that will expire this month. If your little one is particularly ambitious, have him or her find plates that have already expired!

What Day Is Today?

As you drive, have your child review the days of the week by associating them with your weekly routine. "We are driving to the daycare center for the first time this week, so it must be Monday. What comes after Monday?" ("Tuesday!") "What happens on Tuesday that doesn't happen on any other day?" ("On Tuesday we go to the park to play.")

Shapes

From the time your child is born, he or she is surrounded by objects of every size and shape imaginable. The child quickly discovers similarities: a ball is round, an orange is round. He or she later learns that these objects have names—circle, square, triangle.

When your child becomes interested in a particular object, use this as an opportunity to discuss shapes. For instance, if the object is a ball, you would describe it as round. The word "round" would lead to a discussion of circles, and before you know it, your little one will be looking for circles everywhere you go.

Help your child associate each shape with a familiar object. Balls are round, boxes are square, rectangles look like refrigerators, and the sail on a sailboat is shaped like a triangle.

At Home

Beautiful, Colorful Shapes

Draw a square on a sheet of paper, then have your youngster trace over it with a marker or colored pencil. Next, draw a square made of broken lines and ask your child to "connect the dots." Once the youngster has managed to trace these squares successfully, he or she may be ready to face that big, blank sheet of paper.

At Home

Stencil Skills

Use stencils to draw perfect circles, squares, and hearts. Have your little one color or decorate the shapes before cutting them out, then encourage the child to build pictures out of these shapes, such as robots from squares or snowmen from circles.

Homemade Stencils

Let your child trace cookie cutters or the bottoms of cans and boxes. You might even cut stencil shapes out of cardboard for your child to keep with his or her art materials.

Spaghetti Shapes

Set out some construction paper and a box of uncooked spaghetti, and let the shape-making begin! When the masterpiece is complete, have your child glue the spaghetti on the paper. Your little one can use crayons or watercolors to add the finishing touches.

Break Out Those Building Blocks!

Each block is a different shape, and your child can put them together to form other shapes. Can your little one build a pyramid out of squares?

Shape Bingo

You know the drill! Make cards with lots of different shapes on them, call out shape names, and have your little one use pennies to cover the correct shapes.

The Food Pyramid

Entice picky eaters with the food pyramid! "Johnny, what shape is that waffle? Does your egg look more like a circle or a rectangle? The plate is round—what shape does it remind you of?" Cut an orange into crescents, toast into triangles, and give your little one square pats of butter to spread on his or her bread.

At Home

A Plate Full of Shapes

At snack time, put out rectangular crackers, triangles of cheese, round pepperoni slices—the possibilities are endless. Let your little one make his or her own snack using one of each shape.

Better yet, let your youngster in on the fun and plan a triangular meal! Serve tomato wedges, pizza slices, triangular sandwiches, or pyramids of cheese.

Puzzles

Puzzles teach children how shapes fit together. For kids who are new to shapes, buy or make simple puzzles with only four or five pieces. As your child progresses, make the puzzles more and more difficult. Be careful not to make them too hard, however, or you may turn your youngster off shapes entirely.

Play Dough and Modeling Clay

Roll the dough to form balls and ovals, and use cookie cutters and plastics knives to cut different shapes. Ambitious children might put these shapes together to create buildings or people.

At Home

Styrofoam Squiggles

Strange shapes are especially intriguing to young minds, so save the styrofoam that comes as packing material in the mail. Glue them together to make a picture or statue, or string them with a needle and thread to make a necklace. Count them, paint them, sort them—let your child's creativity be the guide.

Super-Sized Shape Books

Make a giant shape book with separate pages for circles, squares, triangles, hearts—every shape you can think of. Fill these pages with shape drawings and shapes cut out of magazines. For a truly original art book, add some geometric "paintings" to the cover!

Shape Painting

Dip different objects into paint and press them onto white paper. Try a comb, a marble, a sponge, a toy car. Make handprints and footprints, elbow prints and nose prints—use your imagination!

At Home

A Shape-Cutting Marathon

Give kids paper and scissors and watch them go! See how many different shapes they can cut out. For more advanced youngsters, practice making snowflakes or paper chains.

New Dimensions

Cut out a picture of a cereal box from a newspaper or magazine, then take the actual cereal box out of the cupboard. Let your child compare the picture to the three-dimensional object.

Leaf Collection

When autumn rolls around, gather up fallen leaves wherever you go. After a week, take a look at all the different shapes you've found. Press the leaves in a book, or get out some crayons and wax paper for a leaf-rubbing weekend.

On the Town

At the Art Museum

Help your child look for shapes within paintings and sketches at your local art museum. Do any of the shapes come together to form an image, such as a person or a building?

Get in Shape!

Take a long walk, pointing out squares and triangles as you go. You might even play "I Spy" or make up other little games along the way.

Lounging in the Sun

Gaze at the clouds on a lazy afternoon. Notice how petunias have a different shape than oak leaves. Wade in a stream or swimming pool, then walk around on the concrete and look at your footprints. Let your child explore the many shapes around you.

Playtime in the Park

When your little one meets up with friends at the park, challenge them to a game of Body Shapes. Let them lay on the grass and put their bodies together to make a square, triangle, circle, and heart.

Scavenger Hunt

Kids get bored tagging along while grown-ups run errands, so have little ones hunt for shapes along the way! Need a circle? Look for pennies on the ground. A rectangle? Pick up a book at the library. Can't find a star? Buy a star fruit at the supermarket!

In the Car

On the Lookout

Have kids call out the shapes of the road signs you pass. They'll see rectangular city signs, yield signs shaped like triangles, and stop signs shaped liked octagons. See who can find the most unusual shape!

Magnetic Shapes

Bring shape magnets and a magnetic board along on your next car trip. Have your youngster name the shapes, sort them, and create pictures out of all the different pieces.

I Spy . . .

Turn "I Spy" into a geometrical challenge! When you come to a stoplight, say "I spy, with my little eye, something round." Is it a tire? The stoplight? The steering wheel? See if your child can guess the object before the light turns green.

On the Road Again

On a long ride with impatient kids, brainstorm objects that are of the same shape. Balls, tires, pennies, gumballs, marbles, doorknobs. . . . Can you think of any circles that belong in the supermarket? At the beach?

Counting Shapes

Count the triangles you see along the road. Better yet, count only the triangles that are inside the car. This is a great game for a quick trip to the post office!

Colors

Although children are fascinated with colors, they often have trouble remembering the names of some colors. Parents will repeat over and over again that the sky is blue, but with many kids, it just doesn't seem to stick. It's as if they have a mental block when it comes to memorizing the names of certain colors.

Don't feel dismayed if your little one fails to recall the color of a fire truck or the shade of the sun—it's perfectly natural to have trouble at this age. Give your child time, patience, and practice. Your youngster will learn the colors soon enough.

At Home

Sweet Incentives

Teach your child to match colors. Place two red M&Ms, two green M&Ms, and two blue M&Ms on the table. Mix them up, then have your son or daughter match each M&M to its mate. Afterward, your little one can munch away on a job well done!

For kids who get enough sugar as it is, use green, red, and purple grapes instead of M&Ms.

Crayons

Keep crayons on hand for emergency art projects. The more your child draws with colors, the sooner he or she will learn their names.

At Home

Color Talk

Never miss a chance to talk about colors. When your child asks for his or her bear at bedtime, ask "What color is Bear?" If he or she wants grape juice for breakfast, talk about the color purple.

If a child hears "the grass is green" often enough, he or she will eventually memorize it. Then, when your little one sees a pine tree, he or she will relate it to the grass—and the word "green."

It's "Red" Week!

Hang up red pictures, draw with red crayons, cook red food (like spaghetti with lots of sauce and an apple for dessert), and point out every red object you see. Talk about other colors, too, but keep your child focused on red. Next week, pick another color.

What's Your Favorite Color?

Some children find it easier to remember colors by associating them with people. Have your child quiz family members about their favorite colors.

At Home

A Color Book

Collect eight different colors of construction paper. Your youngster will have a color book just waiting to come alive! Help your little one cut color photographs out of magazines. Glue the yellow pictures on the yellow page, the green pictures on the green, and so forth. By the time the masterpiece is complete, your child will be able to rattle off every color in the book!

Lavender, Copper, and Silver

Many children are intrigued by the more unusual colors, so introduce these colors as they appear in your child's environment. For example, when your youngster picks up a penny, explain that pennies are copper colored. Sometimes children find the "hard" colors easiest to remember.

Who is Roy G. Biv?

Your child can learn all the colors of the rainbow with this simple mnemonic for Red, Orange, Yellow, Green, Blue, Indigo, Violet. See if your child can draw a rainbow using all the right colors.

At Home

Mix and Match

Add a little color to your morning routine! When your son or daughter gets dressed in the morning, explain that he or she will be wearing red socks because they match the red in his or her shirt and go well with black pants. Children love to mix and match colors, so let your youngster help pick out clothes whenever possible.

Painting Practice

Have young artists name the colors as they paint, and encourage them to experiment by mixing a few colors together. What do yellow and blue make? What can we mix to make black? Your youngster will enjoy the colors as much as the mess.

Sidewalk Art

Brighten up the sidewalk with colored chalk! Draw a line and ask your little one to guess what color it is. If the child gets it right, let him or her draw while *you* guess. Chalk drawings are a great opportunity for young artists to review their colors.

At Home

What Would Colors Taste Like?

We associate colors with temperatures and emotions, why not flavors? Ask your little one to describe what the color blue would taste like, smell like, feel like. Be prepared for an original—and perhaps poetic—response.

Character Colors

Barney is purple, Big Bird is yellow. When reading books or watching television, quiz your child on the colors of each character.

Blue Bath Water?

Add food coloring to your child's bath water! Believe it or not, food coloring won't stain your child's skin (or the bathtub). If your child has a tendency to disappear around bath time, just watch how fast he or she jumps into a tub full of blue! When the primary colors get boring, let your child see what happens when you mix blue and yellow!

On the Town

Sports, Sports, and More Sports!

Visit your local sports apparel store and point out that each sports team has a different color combination. Young sports fans will quickly learn to associate colors with teams.

Colors around Town

What color is the daycare center? What colors are on the outside of the barbershop? How about the exit sign at the movie theater? Show your little one that many colors are used consistently throughout the neighborhood, and he or she will quickly learn to identify them.

Hiking through the Woods

Go on long nature walks at different times of the year. In the spring, all sorts of colorful flowers begin to poke through the ground. Summers bring bright yellow sunlight and lots of blue sky. Leaves change to red, yellow, and brown in the fall, and white snow frosts the trees in the winter. Look at the world around you, and ask your little one to point out which colors have changed since last season.

In the Car

Colors Good Enough to Eat

On the way to the supermarket, brainstorm orange foods. Ask your little one to list all the orange foods he or she can think of: pumpkins, oranges, carrots, cheddar cheese—then move on to harder colors, like yellow and blue.

Road Colors

Have your child call out the colors of signs and streetlights he or she sees on the road. What does red mean? How about yellow or green?

Rainy-Day Colors

From blue upholstery to bright yellow rain-coats, your child could probably find all the colors of the rainbow without even looking out the window.

Chapter 5

Community

As your child grows older, he or she will travel to new lands, make friends from different countries, and feel the effects of our government's legislation. Children will spend a lifetime learning about our country's place in this great big world, and the sooner they start, the better.

Each day brings many, many opportunities to discuss world events, citizenship, and the status of our country. Jump on events as they happen and take the time to discuss them with your child. Your youngster will learn to take an interest in happenings around the world and, hopefully, become more receptive to news that most kids would consider boring.

At Home

World at Your Fingertips

Familiarize your little one with basic maps by helping the child make a map of his or her bedroom. Draw an outline of the room and have your youngster draw the furniture in the appropriate places. Label the door, the windows, each piece of furniture, and—voila!—your child has designed his or her first map.

Try boosting your youngster's map skills by hiding a special treasure somewhere in the house. Draw a simple map, mark the spot with a great big X, and send your youngster on a treasure hunt!

Eventually you will introduce "real" maps for your youngster to read. Don't worry about more advanced ideas like topography or converting miles to inches. Stick with simple maps and simple concepts, focusing on only the most basic map-reading skills.

Globe Trotters

Globes resemble children's favorite toys—balls! Give your little one a beach ball that resembles a globe, and let the child explore the shapes and colors. Don't be afraid to name the continents and oceans—your child may even memorize a few of them. Distinguish north from south and east from west. Daydream about far away lands. Travel the globe together.

At Home

Travel the World

Since you can't take your child to all the places he or she will want to see, grab some travel brochures and bring new and interesting sights to your child instead! You might also write to state travel bureaus for information on local tourist attractions.

Suppertime Geography

A place mat bearing a map of the United States or the state in which you live is a great way to familiarize your little one with maps. While your child waits for supper, he or she can look at all the shapes and colors, and maybe even locate a town or two.

Even Grown-Ups Have Rules

Cities make rules in order to keep everyone safe and healthy, just like your family. "Walk in the house," "Tell your parents when you go outside," and "Be nice to each other" might sound like house rules, but they're not that different from "Follow the speed limit" and "Be kind to neighbors." You may want to touch on laws and how they help people to live and work together, but basic rules and niceties are enough for now. The ideas of sharing and caring for each other are more appropriate at this age than a lengthy discussion of taxes and legislation.

At Home

Pursue the News

Look through the paper every day for pictures and stories that may be of interest to kids—an article about a local children's play, a lost animal that finds its way home, or a little league team forming in town, for example. Show your child the sports section, weather forecasts, movie selections, pets for sale—there's bound to be at least one section that will interest your child.

Write Your Own Newspaper

Have your child review newsworthy events that recently occurred in your family or neighborhood. Your youngster can dictate simple sentences while you write down his or her words. Afterward, let the child go back and draw the illustrations. Your little one will end up with a collection of stories to treasure for a lifetime.

Daily News

Although some news isn't suitable for little eyes, there are news programs made especially for kids, and parts of the local news may have stories that are both interesting and appropriate. Watch for upcoming news items and call your child over to watch when they come on. During a snowstorm, watch the weather to learn more about what's happening in your immediate area. Have a little sports fan on your hands? Catch the score during the sports highlights.

At Home

Broadcast News

Let your child stage his or her very own news show. Your little one can report on family events or neighborhood gossip. Expect a dramatic performance!

Customs around the World

Read about distant lands, make some simple costumes, and let your child role-play people from different cultures.

A Taste of China

Turn a typical Tuesday night supper into a Chinese celebration. Serve Chinese take-out, or cook up some of your own delicacies. Set out chop sticks, decorate the table, and dress the part. Try a different country at least one night a month, tasting its foods, customs, and history.

Coin Collections

Start a collection of coins from around the world. Place the prettiest coins under a very thin piece of paper and rub lightly over them with a crayon or pencil. An image of the coin will appear right before your child's eyes!

At Home

Made in Taiwan

Have your child check his or her belongings to see what country they were made in. Your youngster probably has toys that were made in China, clothing from the Philippines, and a tape recorder from Japan.

Pen Pals

With a pen pal, your son or daughter will not only make a new friend, he or she will learn about a different part of the world. Have your child write to a relative who lives far away. Call your old college roommate and see if his or her child would be interested in writing back and forth with yours. If you belong to a religious organization, ask if they can help connect your youngster with another child with similar interests. With a little persistence, you will find the perfect pen pal for your child.

Postcards from around the World

Have friends and family send postcards when they go on vacation, and help your child find their vacation spots on a map. By the time your little one starts school, he or she will have a formidable postcard collection!

At Home

Family Tree

Starting with your immediate family, show your little one how all of his or her relatives are related, telling a little bit about each person's history. "Aunt Wendy is my sister. She married Uncle Steve, so he is my brother-in-law. They are your aunt and uncle." "Your great-grandmother's name was Helen. She came all the way to America from Scotland." Your little one will be thrilled to learn about his or her ancestors.

This Is Your Life

To help your little one understand the concepts of time and chronological order, draw a time line of your child's life. Start with the day he or she was born. Include the child's first word, first step, and other momentous occasions, like birthdays and family vacations. When the time line is complete, let your child draw the illustrations.

Time Capsule

Help your youngster collect a few items that represent his or her life—crayons, books, a bike, and so forth. Put the small objects into a sealable container (with photographs of the large objects), and invite family members to add their own treasures to the collection. Make a list of the objects, seal the time capsule, and bury it in the backyard. Don't forget to set a date for the container to be reopened!

On the Town

Travel

Visiting actual historic sights will teach your little one more than any classroom possibly could. After all, the best way to learn about new places is to see them firsthand! Encourage your child to keep a journal on each trip, even if it's just a series of drawings. This little book will jiggle memories in years to come.

Day Tripper

Call your city hall or tourist information to find out which sights they recommend to people visiting your hometown. This way, you can keep costs down and learn about your community at the same time!

Community Workers

Make a list of all the service workers you can think of, then discuss what they do and how they help your town. Tour the courthouse or local hospital, and take a few minutes to talk to a police officer or fire fighter, letting your child ask some questions. Make a point of meeting as many of these dedicated workers as you can.

On the Town

Local History

Research your hometown together at the local library or talk with older residents in your community. Encourage your child to ask questions about what life was like in his or her town long, long ago.

Skip the Hamburger

Try a restaurant with an international flair! Introduce your youngster to a Chinese buffet, Mexican meal, or Italian cuisine. Look at the pictures on restaurant walls, and talk about how much fun it would be to visit those countries!

Historical Holidays

Help your child understand Presidents' Day or Memorial Day by visiting museums and cemeteries. Read books about the holidays and discuss why we celebrate them.

On the Town

Community Spirit

Help your child join a fund-raiser or a service club. You'll be surprised at how much a little one can do!

Pick a Favorite Country

Have your child pick a country, then help him or her learn as much about it as possible. Look in the encyclopedia, check out the Internet, and cut photographs and articles out of magazines. Once you've gathered all the information, help your youngster turn it into a book!

Stamp Collection

Buy your youngster stamps from the local post office, and be sure to watch for new series coming out. Before you know it, your little one will be collecting stamps from around the world.

Nine to Five

Bring your child to work so he or she can see what you do all day long. Explain that people all over the world work hard to provide products and services that keep their communities going. What does your youngster want to do when he or she grows up?

In the Car

Patriotic Songs

Pop in a tape of patriotic music and expose your little one to our country's songs, symbols, and history.

American Heroes

You don't have to be a social studies teacher to share a few facts about George Washington, Betsy Ross, or Benjamin Franklin. Introductory tidbits may be just enough to get your child interested in learning more.

Red, White, and Blue

Look for the colors of the flag as you drive and talk about their significance in our country's history.

History in the Making

As you drive past the courthouse, give a brief explanation of what goes on inside. Talk about prominent figures in your community. Quiz your child on the name of the president and mention significant events that are happening today in America.

Chapter 6

Science

A young child is like a sponge just waiting to soak up information. If the most popular words in your household are "who," "how," and "why," you may have a natural born scientist on your hands. Try not to get annoyed with a little one's constant questioning. This curiosity will guide the child as he or she explores the earth, solar system, plants, animals, and all the things that make up the world around us.

At Home

Wonders of the Kitchen

"How do you make ice cubes?" "Where do the pipes under the sink lead?" "How come milk is runny and bread isn't?" Take the time to answer your youngster's questions, no matter how silly they may seem.

If you can't answer your little one's question right then and there, come back to it later when you have more time. "I'm cooking right now so I don't have time to explain how they make flour. I'll try to explain it to you as soon as we're finished with supper. Tomorrow, we'll go to the library and find some books on grains and farming so I can tell you the whole story." These three little sentences will mean a lot to your child.

Science Experiments

It is often easier to demonstrate how something works than to describe it. You can explain the concept of melting over and over again, but bring a snowball in the house or leave a Popsicle on the counter, and your youngster will see the melting process firsthand. "Showing" your child takes a little more time and effort, but if you truly want your little one to understand, experiments are the best way to go.

At Home

Bathtub Games

- Give your youngster different objects to experiment with in the tub. "Will the water in this tall cup fit in this short, round bowl?" "Will this bar of soap sink or float?"

- Put an ice cube in warm bath water and see what happens.

- As the tub fills up, pour a capful of liquid bubble bath in the water. Wow! How did those bubbles get in there?

- What happens when you put a dry sponge in the water?

- Why does your skin wrinkle after you play in the tub for a while?

- Pick up a bar of soap and ask your child to use all of his or her five senses to learn about this object. "How does it smell?" "What does it feel like? Is it smooth or rough?" "Does it make noise?" "Can you eat it?" "What color is it?"

At Home

A Taste of Science

The ability to sort and classify is an essential one for budding scientists, so start with simple questions. Is your little one having anything sweet or sour for lunch? Is popcorn salty or bitter? What does a lemon taste like?

Magnets

Give your little one a magnet and let your child experiment on his or her own. Will it stick to the wall? The refrigerator door? What happens when you turn the magnet over? Your child will quickly catch on to the power of magnetism.

Energy Conservation

Little kids can make a big difference in conserving water and energy. Explain why conservation is so important, then show what children can do to help. Teach them to turn off the lights when they leave a room. While they're brushing their teeth, they can shut off the water. Remind them to shut the refrigerator door while they decide what to eat, and invite them to help sort the recycling.

At Home

Natural Wonders

Watch the birds and squirrels to find out where they live. What do they eat? Do birds that eat seeds have the same shape beaks as the birds that eat insects? How do squirrels seem to communicate with each other?

Adopt a Pet

If you can't keep a dog or cat in your home, consider a parakeet, fish, guinea pig, hamster, chameleon, or hermit crab. Caring for a pet is an excellent opportunity to study an animal in its own environment. Teach your little one how to feed his or her pet and keep it healthy and clean. And don't forget about outdoor animals—leave out peanuts for the squirrels, seeds for the birds, and salt licks for the deer.

Alternative Animals

If your child would love to have a horse, but it's simply not possible, frame horse pictures, pin horse posters to the walls, or make a horse scrapbook. Children don't have to own an animal to love and learn about it.

At Home

Nocturnal Wonders

Buy a child-size telescope for young stargazers and check out some books about the constellations. Build a campfire or bring a flashlight outdoors and read bedtime stories. Your child will marvel at the moon, the shooting stars, and all the wonderful sounds of the night.

Tending the Garden

An enormous amount of learning can take place in just one growing season, so let your child plant seeds, pull weeds, water flowers and vegetables, and harvest crops.

But don't limit your youngster to an outdoor garden. Give the child a plant to keep and care for in his or her bedroom. Plant some seeds and watch them grow. Stick a carrot top or potato eye in a pot of soil and see what happens after a few days. Your little one might even make a terrarium or rock garden to decorate your house.

Moon in the Sky

Sometimes the moon is full, other times it's just a sliver. Why? Have your child draw the moon every night for two months. Does there seem to be a pattern?

At Home

Details, Details!

Give your child a microscope. He or she will be astonished to see the tiniest details in specimens that are too small to view with the naked eye.

Backyard Bird Watching

Turn a lazy afternoon into a bird-watching expedition! Put out feeders to attract different species, and teach your little one the names of the birds that visit your backyard. Keep a child-level bird book on hand and help your child look up the birds you see on nature walks.

Bubble Festival

There are tons of bubble toys on the market today: motorized blowers, funky wands, giant bubble makers—you name it. Invest in one, or design some bubble makers of your own.

To make bubble solution, use one part dish-washing soap and two parts water. Make wands out of bent wire, dip them in the solution, and blow bubbles galore!

On the Town

The Great Outdoors

Young scientists are thrilled to explore new and interesting places, so investigate caves, lakes, caverns, quarries, ponds, fields, woods, and other new frontiers your child might want to conquer.

Seeking Out Science

Count birds, leaves, or rocks as you wander through the woods; roam your backyard for unusual bugs; and look for seashells along the beach. Nature has an infinite number of plants and animals just waiting to be discovered, but you have to go out and find them.

Beach Bum

Bring spoons, sifters, and measuring cups to the beach or sandbox and help your little one mix water with sand. Explain that wet sand is firmer than dry sand, so it's a little easier to build with. Your youngster can spend the rest of the afternoon "experimenting" with sandcastles.

On the Town

Dinosaurs? Science? You Bet!

Dinosaurs teach us what the earth was like a long, long time ago. Take a trip to the library or the science museum. Together, you and your child will learn about fossils, paleontologists, and much more.

Science in Action

Introduce your youngster to doctors, nurses, teachers, chefs, farmers, and others who rely on science to do their jobs. Show your child that science is more than the study of rocks and chemicals. It is the study of the world around us.

Digging for Earthworms

How far down in the ground do they live? How do they get from one place to another? Do earthworms have eyes? These funny little creatures will inspire plenty of questions, so consider checking out an earthworm book from the library.

On the Town

Childhood Treasures

Children's pockets carry everything from rocks to daisies to frogs. Rather than thwart this love of the outdoors, encourage it by helping your youngster get started on his or her very own research. Start at the library. Remember, when buying or checking out books on a particular subject, make sure they are suited to your child's level. Books that are written for adults are likely to frustrate little ones and cause them to lose interest.

- **Flowers.** Bring a simple flower identification book along on nature walks and look up flower species along the way. Where flowers are abundant, pick some for drying or pressing in a catalog. Encourage your child to touch, smell, and look closely at each flower.

- **Natural souvenirs.** Scour the ground for pinecones, white rocks, flowers, sticks— anything your child takes a liking to. When you get home, put these objects in a treasure chest. Your child can use these treasures later in terrariums, art projects, and decorations. Pinecones will turn into wreaths, bird nests will appear in the den—before you know it, your home will be filled with beautiful reminders of your walks together.

- **Rocks.** If your child likes to bring home rocks, designate a "rock spot" in the basement or garage where he or she can keep them. Visit the library for children's books about rocks, and buy a magnifying glass so your little one can study them in minute detail. Encourage your child to develop his or her own classification system and draw his or her observations. The child might write a story about gems or incorporate little rocks into art projects. By the time your youngster gets to school, he or she may be a little expert on rocks and minerals!

- **Insects.** Many children have a special affection for creeping, crawling, flying things. If they want to start a bug collection, explain that bugs are living creatures and deserve the same respect that all living creatures do. Let them study bugs in their natural environment, without capturing and killing them. If your child wishes, he or she may catch one, study it, and let it go again. Insects that are already dead are free for the taking—use straight pins to mount them on heavy cardboard, then label their names and note where they were found.

On the Town

On the Town

- **Leaves.** Trees provide beauty, shade, oxygen, and homes for many living creatures. To help your child learn more about these magnificent organisms, start a leaf collection. Roam the neighborhood or woods together, picking up the prettiest, most interesting leaves along the way. When you get home, look them up in a leaf book, press them in a catalog, or iron them between two sheets of wax paper. You'll be surprised at how quickly your child will learn to identify trees just by examining the leaves.

In the Car

Pop Quiz!

Ask your child science questions on your next road trip. "Do you think rocks sink or float?" "Why do the leaves change colors?" Use these conversations as a springboard for library research later on.

Just an Observation . . .

As you buckle your little one into his or her car seat, give the child a rock to hold. Have your youngster use his or her five senses to describe the rock as you drive along. Try a different object for each car trip, such as a leaf, pinecone, ice cube, apple, or flower.

Call of the Wild

Call out the names of animals as you drive. What is the most common animal you see along the road? What is the least common? See who can spot the most animal species along the way.

Weather Wonder

Is it sunny outside? Does it look like rain? Can your little one take a guess at the temperature? Each time you get in the car, have your child draw the weather. Be sure to guess what tomorrow's weather will be like, too!

Chapter 7

Safety, Health, and Hygiene

Safety, health, and hygiene are just as important as the ABCs. Instill good habits from the very start, and health education will seem almost effortless as your youngster grows older. By the time your little one starts school, the child will have learned basic manners and habits that will keep him or her safe, happy, and healthy.

At Home

Appearance Makes a Difference

Regular baths, frequent shampoos, and clean clothes make kids feel as good as they look. Help your little one take pride in his or her appearance. You might even let the child help pick out his or her clothes for the day (although you'll need to explain what matches and what doesn't). If you're short on time, pick out two outfits and let your child choose one.

Proper Hygiene

Make a ritual out of proper hygiene, and these habits will last for a lifetime. Help or remind children to:

- Wash their hands before meals and after using the bathroom.

- Cover their mouth when they sneeze or cough.

- Brush their teeth at least twice a day.

- Keep themselves neat and clean.

- Bathe regularly.

At Home

Mind Your Manners

Remind your youngster to use polite words and phrases in everyday conversation, such as "please," "thank you," and "excuse me." Emphasize good phone manners, and drill your child on how to behave when he or she meets someone new. When your little one starts school, all these good manners will make a great impression.

Time to Get Dressed!

If your child can play dress-up, he or she is ready to learn how to pull on pants and a tee shirt in the morning. Help your little one along if it seems necessary, but encourage the child to do as much as he or she can. Yes, there will be backward shirts and twisted socks, but for the most part, youngsters who can dress themselves have conquered a major childhood hurdle. Let your little one take pride in this accomplishment.

Chores

Once your child can get dressed alone, he or she is ready to take some responsibility for his or her surroundings. Making the bed and tidying the bedroom are reasonable expectations of young children. They won't do a perfect job, of course, but it's the effort that counts. Praise your little one's work—and resist the urge to throw back the sheets and start all over again.

At Home

TV Time-Out

You would think that children get enough exercise running around the house, but an alarming number of kids are woefully out of shape. There's no need to start calisthenics, however; simply turn off the television and join your little one outside to ride a bike, play ball, or take a walk. And remember, if you expect your child to exercise, you need to get in shape yourself. When your son or daughter sees your commitment to fitness, he or she will follow your example.

Turn On That Radio and DANCE!

Rainy days are a great excuse for indoor exercise. Pop in a favorite tape and watch your little one boogie down. Afterward, lay some masking tape on the carpet and play hopscotch. Goal-oriented parents might have children help sweep the floor, clean out the closet, or deliver clean laundry to the proper bedrooms. Light household chores will bring children one step closer to fitness.

At Home

Healthy Habits

Most little kids are old enough to learn the difference between foods that are good for them and foods that aren't. Make a food chart to help your little one discriminate between the two. Teach the youngster to eat a balanced diet, and when food looks unappealing, encourage the child to try a bite anyway.

Of course, the most effective way to instill good eating habits is to eat plenty of fruits and vegetables yourself. Be patient with little ones. In time, most children will acquire a taste for foods you never thought they would try.

Fun Foods

To entice a reluctant eater, peel a banana, hold it lengthwise, add four tiny pretzel sticks to each side, and—voila!—a caterpillar. Or try pouring pancake batter into a metal cookie cutter on a skillet. You might add carrot eyes and potato legs to roast beef, or grate raw vegetables into your child's meatloaf or hamburger before cooking. Your little one will get his or her vitamins and minerals without even knowing it! There are hundreds of ways to shape, mince, and prepare foods to make them more appetizing for children. Use your imagination.

At Home

Safety First

Your child's health and safety are more important than anything else in the world.
Fortunately, if you teach your child basic safety
rules from the start—and are confident that he
or she will practice them—you are further
ahead in the safety game than most.

Sit down with your child and make a few simple house rules together. If your little one can
help make the rules, he or she will be less likely
to break them. Try to steer your child in the
right direction by asking, "What are some
good rules we can make for bath time?" "Can
you think of some rules for when we go to the
supermarket?"

Consider outdoor rules, too. Can your son or
daughter take the dog out? Is it okay to leave
the yard and go play at the neighbor's?

Try to find positive ways to express these rules,
such as "Walk in the house" (instead of "Don't
run"), "Furniture is for sitting on (not jumping
on)," and "Use inside voices indoors; save outside voices for outdoors." State the more
urgent rules directly:

- **Never taste anything without asking
  your Mom or Dad first.** Parents, of
  course, are still responsible for keeping
  medicines and cleaning solutions out of
  the reach of children.

At Home

- **Never use the stove or a kitchen appliance without the help of a grown-up.** Parents should talk about kitchen safety every time they bake or cook with their children. Teach kids how to avoid hot water, sharp knives, hot burners, electricity, and other dangers lurking in the kitchen. In the meantime, use only the back burners on the stove, so small hands won't get burned when they wander up top to see what's for supper.

- **Do not put anything into electrical outlets.** Although some children are capable of plugging a cord into the wall, kids ought to leave this to the grown-ups. Teach children that even though electricity is helpful, it is also very dangerous—if we use it wrong, it can burn us.

- **Be careful when turning on the faucet.** Hot water injures thousands of children each year. Teach your youngster the difference between the hot and cold handle on sinks, tubs, and showers. Even if your child understands the difference, let grown-ups be in charge of faucets.

  Each time your child needs to take a bath or wash his or her hands, turn on the water yourself and check the temperature before the child touches it. If someone runs the laundry machine or flushes a toilet somewhere in the house, it can change the water temperature drastically.

On the Town

Exercise

Take your child to a swimming pool or bowling alley. Go skating, roller blading, horseback riding. Visit the recreational center and play tennis or racquetball. Hike through the woods.

You might also guide your child toward a group sport, such as little league, ballet, or soccer. But don't rely on the coach or instructor to teach good sportsmanship—encourage your child to stick with it, even if he or she isn't the best in the group. After all, having fun is the number one priority.

Taking Pride in Healthy Habits

When visiting a restaurant, order nutritious food and help your child wash his or her hands before the meal arrives. Show your youngster that good hygiene is important no matter where you are.

Snack Attack

Hit the supermarket on a Friday afternoon and stock up on healthy snacks for the weekend.

Hospital Tour

Peek in on the newborns and peruse the gift shop. If your little one ever needs to visit the hospital, he or she will be on familiar turf, making the entire experience a little less traumatic.

In the Car

Buckle Up!

Every time you get in the car, be sure to buckle your child's seat belt as well as your own. This will become a habit that will last a lifetime.

The Safety Game

Quiz your child on common health and safety rules as you drive. "What should you do if you feel a sneeze coming on?" "What should you do before you cross the street?" These little review sessions will keep safety rules fresh in your child's mind.

Copilots

Kids get bored riding along in the car, so let them be active participants from time to time—as long as they obey the rules:

- Stay buckled.

- Don't distract the driver.

- Be on the look-out for potential hazards.

"Copilots" are far more helpful to drivers than restless children, and kids are always happy to help Mom or Dad.

Pedestrian Safety

As you pass people walking down the street, have your child determine if they are walking safely. If not, what should they do differently?

Chapter 8

Holiday
Activities

Holidays are special opportunities for children to show off their skills. Watch their imaginations run wild! Together, you and your child will find plenty of opportunities to count, write, measure, experiment, and learn during the most exciting days of the year.

Winter Holidays

ABC Festivities

Trace large letters on holiday wrapping paper, cut them out, and put them in an original holiday letter book.

Cookie Time

Bake holiday letter cookies and spell out words on the cookie tray. A tray full of HAPPY HOLIDAYS won't last long with little ones around! When they ask for a cookie, let them pick out a letter—by name. Help your child spell out new words with the cookies that remain.

Snow Day

Fill a squirt gun with colored water, take it outside on a winter day, and write letters in the snow!

Happy Holidays!

Encourage your child to send cards to friends and relatives. If your youngster isn't quite ready to sign his or her name, the first letter will do. Otherwise, you can take the child's hand in your own and "help" him or her write the name.

Winter Holidays

Parent's Little Helper

Ask your youngster to help with your shopping list! Your little one can count the number of people you need to buy gifts for and how many stores you will need to visit.

It's That Time of Year Again . . .

To many children, winter holidays mean one thing—presents! No doubt your little one will have a mental wish list, so help the youngster draw or write his or her wishes down on paper. Afterward, have your child count the gifts that he or she has asked for.

TV Time

After watching a holiday special on television, write down your child's words as he or she explains what the program was about, or have the child draw a favorite scene from the show.

New Year's Resolutions

Help your child make a list of resolutions for the new year. Just think, by this time next year, your little one may be able to write out his or her own list!

'Tis the Season to Be Baking

Let your little one measure and count the ingredients while you bake. At the end of the night, count the number of cookies, brownies, and pastries you made together.

Winter Holidays

Holiday Countdown

Starting on December 1st, hang up one decoration each day, cross off days on the calendar, or mail one holiday card every afternoon. Find a unique way to count down the days, and make it a custom in your home.

Winter Wonderland

Take a winter drive and count the houses with outdoor lights. Finish up with a cup of hot chocolate—and don't forget to count the marshmallows!

Loose Change?

Have your little one count the number of quarters he or she drops in the Salvation Army bin. Your child will learn the true meaning of "season of giving."

Number Skating

Take your little one to the ice rink and skate numbers in the ice! Practice shapes and letters as well.

Winter Geometry

How many shapes can your child build with snow? Sure, snowballs are easy, but how about snow triangles? Make a winter "shape garden," and see how many different shapes you can come up with.

Winter Holidays

World Tour

Visit the library for books that will teach your child about holiday customs and traditions around the world.

Happy (Chinese) New Year!

Go to the library to find the right date (and the right animal) for a Chinese New Year party. If February brings the Year of the Tiger, invite all the neighborhood kids over for fortune cookies, Chinese lanterns, and plenty of tiger paraphernalia.

Holiday Swap

Whether you celebrate Christmas, Hanukkah, Kwanzaa, or Winter Solstice, find a friend who celebrates a different holiday and trade celebrations! Have your child invite the friend to share your holiday in exchange for an invitation to share his or hers. Your little one will learn about new religions and traditions firsthand.

Mail from around the World

Count the holiday cards that come in the mail, tack a map to the wall, and mark where each card was sent from. Don't forget to save the stamps!

Winter Holidays

Once Upon a Time . . .

Ask your little one to tell or draw a story about how your holiday might have started. What does the holiday mean? When and where was the first celebration? Who started it and why? What kinds of food did they eat? Encourage your youngster to use his or her imagination. If the child is interested, head for the library and look for books to explain how your holiday actually originated and compare these with your child's version. Are there any similarities?

Winter Solstice

Watch the sun rise and set on the shortest day of the year. Tomorrow, the days will start getting longer again!

Sorting the Mail

Have the child separate the holiday cards according to the pictures. Some cards will have snow, animals, trees, bells—the hard part comes when cards have both animals *and* snow. Which category do they belong in? Watch how your little one solves this dilemma.

The Great Snowball Experiment

Have your youngster bring a snowball indoors, place it in a liquid measuring cup, and guess how much water there will be when it melts. Did he or she guess right? Next, pour the water in a pan and turn on the stove (don't let your child do this alone). Where did all the water go?

Snowflake Inspection

Have your child use a magnifying glass to look closely at the snowflakes that fall on his or her coat. Do any of the snowflakes look alike? Count how many points there are on each snowflake. Are there more six-pointed flakes or five-pointed flakes? What do snowflakes seem to be made of?

Candle Patrol

If your family lights candles during the holidays, ask your little one to make sure they are all blown out before he or she goes to bed. If the candles are left burning, they could start a fire! Blowing out the candles is a big responsibility, but little kids will be eager to take it on.

Winter Holidays

Valentine's Day

Have a Heart

Spend an afternoon cutting out red and pink hearts. Count all of your hearts at the end, and give them away to friends and family.

Valentine's Day Cards

Make a list of friends and relatives the child wants to send Valentines to, then help your youngster sign each card. Address the envelopes for your little one, but let the child participate as much as possible.

A List of Loving Words

Make a list of common Valentine's Day words and help your child look them up in the dictionary. Invite the youngster to copy down his or her favorite word (and its definition, if he or she is more advanced).

Letters from the Heart

Decorate heart-shaped cookies with letters of the alphabet. Your child can give one cookie to each friend whose name begins with that letter.

Valentine's Day

Candy Calculations

Have children count the chocolates in a box of candy, then let them count the number of chocolates they can have for dessert. Kids really like this one!

Kiss Math

How much is one plus one? Kiss your little one on the forehead and say "(Kiss) plus (kiss) is (kiss kiss)!" The child won't actually learn how to add, but he or she can count the kisses!

A Million Ways to Say "I Love You"

Kids are quick to soak up new words, so help your little one learn to say "I love you" in another language. Better yet, go to the library and find out how to say it in as many languages as you can.

St. Patrick's Day

Who Are the Irish?

Make a special trip to the library for books on the Irish and St. Patrick's Day.

Shamrock Stencils

Draw a large shamrock on cardboard, cut it out, and let your little one trace shamrocks on green construction paper. Fill the house with your child's decorations.

Walking Green

Take a walk outdoors and see how many green objects you and your child can find. Be sure to check the grass for leprechauns!

St. Patrick's Day Tee Shirts

On a plain white shirt, help your child trace shamrock stencils with green fabric paint— your little one will be delighted to wear his or her artwork all over town!

Green, Green, Green!

Prepare a green meal with your little one! Try green linguini, stuffed green peppers, or green beans. Drink lime punch and have pistachio cake or lime Jell-O for dessert.

Fourth of July

Library Lessons

Take your child to the library for books about the Fourth of July. Afterward, have your little one make a book or draw pictures of what he or she has learned.

Seeing Stars

While teaching your little one to count to fifty, count the stars on the flag, then discuss what these stars represent.

Fireworks

Let your child squirt glue onto paper, then sprinkle beautiful bursts of gold, red, and silver glitter on top before it dries.

Picnic Fun

Celebrate the Fourth of July with a picnic! Sing patriotic songs, count the ants that come to visit, and decorate your table with red, white, and blue.

Floral Fireworks

Next time you go for a walk, bring home some Queen Anne's lace for a special fireworks display! Dip the flower in tempera paint, press it onto paper, sit back, and watch the show.

Fourth of July

Patriotic Garden

Help your child choose a variety of red, white, and blue flowers. Plant them in a garden and let your little one tend to them all summer long.

Dining on Red, White, and Blue

For a successful pre-fireworks celebration, ask your little one to help plan a red, white, and blue meal! It will take some creativity (and maybe a little food coloring), but your little one will love it.

Star-Spangled Fun

Teach kids the national anthem! Children love to sing, so take advantage of this natural enthusiasm to share important images and events from our country's history.

Melting Pot

Think of all the nationalities that make up the melting pot—some lived here at the start, others came over on the Mayflower, still others came from all around the world. Where did your family come from? Discuss your family's origins and encourage the child to write a story or draw pictures about his or her ancestors living or arriving in the United States.

Fourth of July

A Picnic Poll

Poll taking is an excellent way for youngsters to learn about other people's attitudes. At your Fourth of July picnic, have your little one ask each picnicker to name a favorite picnic food, favorite firecracker color, and what he or she likes best about July 4th.

Dress the Part

Let your little one show off our nation's colors—help him or her pick out a special outfit to wear for the big day.

Invent a Country

If your youngster could have his or her very own country, what would it look like? Who would live there? Would there be a leader? Talk about the weather, land, people, food, and animals. What would life be like? Would kids have a bedtime? What rules would they have to follow? Have your little one draw his or her own flag. What do the colors and symbols represent? Take this opportunity to compare your little one's imaginary country with our own. Are there any similarities?

Halloween

Horrible, Ghastly, Scary Letters

When it's Halloween, even letters can sound spooky! This is a great time to introduce letters that say their name. Practice writing O-o-o-o on paper. (A ghost?) Or maybe E-e-e-e. (A screeching door?)

Boo!

Make scary decorations to hang throughout the house. Write simple words on these, like "boo," "ghost," and "cat."

Pumpkin with a Twist

Instead of carving faces in pumpkins, carve letters! Light a candle inside and turn off the lights. Look how the letters glow in the dark!

Black on White

Write letters on black construction paper with white chalk, add some Halloween stickers, and post them around the house.

Pumpkin Seeds

Have your child guess how many seeds are in a pumpkin. After you're done carving, count the seeds—did your child guess right? How close did he or she come? Save those pumpkin seeds—toasted seeds make a great October snack, and you can even save raw seeds for planting in the spring.

Halloween

Hunting for Jack-o'-Lanterns

Count the pumpkins in the neighborhood. Are there more scary faces or funny faces this year?

Trick-or-Treat!

Have young trick-or-treaters count the number of houses they visit. More houses mean more candy, so don't be surprised if they learn to count very high very quickly!

Ghosts and Goblins

Count the trick-or-treaters that come to your door. How many ghosts stopped by this year?

Candy is Dandy

Let your child dump out all of his or her Halloween goodies and count them—twice!

Go Batty!

Halloween means black cats, ghosts, pumpkins, witches, and the most intriguing creature of all—bats. Where do bats live? Can they see? What do they eat? Where do they go in the winter? Your child will have a million questions once he or she gets rolling, so you might want to go to the library and find a book about these mysterious creatures.

Halloween

One for You, One for Me

Have your little one sort and classify his or her Halloween treats. Put the gum in one pile and the chocolate in another, sort them by wrapper color, or let your child devise his or her own classification system.

Halloween Flowers

Take a white carnation and, without detaching the stem, split the stem in half. Place one half in a cup of water filled with orange food coloring, the other in water with brown food coloring. The flower will drink in the different Halloween colors, turning the petals orange and brown!

Halloween

Safety First

Ask your little one to help make up rules for Halloween, like:

- Wear a bright costume when trick-or-treating in the dark.

- Bring a flashlight.

- Never go anywhere with a stranger.

- Don't taste any candy until Mom or Dad makes sure it is safe to eat.

Don't Forget to Brush!

Halloween is a great time to emphasize healthy habits, like:

- No more than four pieces of candy each day.

- Brush your teeth after eating candy.

- No candy before supper.

Thanksgiving

Pumpkin Pie

Bake a pumpkin pie together and let your child count the ingredients.

Count Me In

Give your little one a chance to show off his or her counting skills—let the child count the guests at your Thanksgiving feast.

Sentimental Journey

Have your child ask each guest how many miles he or she travelled to get to your Thanksgiving dinner. Help your child add up the miles and let the little one announce the total at dessert.

The Centerpiece

Help your little one make a turkey out of construction paper, counting the feathers as he or she glues them on. If your child wants to, he or she can practice writing or tracing the numbers on the back of each feather.

Look at All That Food!

Have your child count the number of different foods on the table. (Then try counting the ones he or she will eat!)

Thanksgiving

Holiday Specials

Count the number of TV programs that have Thanksgiving themes. There will be plenty of them, so try not to lose count! Which program was your child's favorite, and why?

Thanksgiving Traditions

Turkey, corn, squash, potatoes, pumpkin pie— all of these foods are indigenous to North America. Explain that the Native Americans ate these foods long before the Pilgrims came over. (Last night's spaghetti, on the other hand, wasn't indigenous—it came from a different country.) Your little one won't understand what "indigenous" means (and probably won't care), but he or she will remember that Thanksgiving foods originated in America.

Helping Hands

Help your child to help others less fortunate. Prepare some food together and drop it off at the nearest soup kitchen. Your little one will enjoy helping with the meal, and he or she will see firsthand that a little charity means a whole lot to people who haven't got enough to eat.

Count Your Blessings

Have your child ask each of your guests what they are thankful for on this Thanksgiving Day.

Birthday

A Birthday Story

Have your little one tell a story about the day he or she was born. Write down the words as your child dictates, and let your youngster draw the illustrations.

Birthday Candles

Have your little one count the candles on his or her birthday cake. Don't forget to make a wish!

Thank-You Notes

Encourage your child to make cards or letters for everyone who bought him or her a gift.

Baby's Birthday

Visit the hospital and look at the newborns. Just think, almost all of those new babies share your little one's birthday!

Plant a Tree

Help your youngster plant a tree on his or her birthday. The whole family can watch the tree grow for years to come.

Birthday

How Quickly They Grow

Photograph your little one in front of a special tree and watch both child and tree grow from year to year. For a more accurate measurement, mark your little one's height on a height chart every year. You'll be amazed at how quickly he or she has grown.

Party Time

Instead of hosting a birthday party in your living room, invite kids to explore a museum, park, or nature sanctuary.

Get a Little, Give a Little

Your child is bound to receive lots of gifts on his or her birthday. Let this day be an opportunity to give something, too. Take your little one to a homeless shelter or battered women's shelter and donate a new toy for the kids. Make giving a birthday tradition.

Conclusion

Teaching a child requires patience and creativity, but the time and effort you put in today will serve your child throughout his or her lifetime. Your youngster will become more independent, confident, and successful in his or her day-to-day activities. Play will be work, but work will be play.

This book contains just a smattering of suggestions to prepare your youngster for success in school and in life. Together, you and your child can think of hundreds of new ideas to make learning fun. Simply take advantage of learning situations as they arise. When you read a book, discuss the pictures. When you take a walk, notice the colors around you. At lunch time, let your youngster open the jar of peanut butter and make his or her own sandwich. It is simple moments like these that will teach your child the most.

Suggested Reading

Children's Books No Home Should Be Without

Berenstain, Stan and Jan. *The Berenstain Bears and the Sitter.* New York: Random House, 1981.

Birdseye, Tom. *Air Mail to the Moon.* New York: The Trumpet Club, 1988.

Bourgeois, Paulette. *Franklin's Blanket.* New York: Scholastic, 1995.

Bridwell, Norman. *Count on Clifford.* New York: Scholastic, 1985.

Brown, Marc. *Arthur's Really Helpful Word Book.* New York: Random House, 1981.

Brown, Marc. *Kiss Hello, Kiss Goodbye.* New York: Random House, 1977.

Butler, Dori Hillestad. *The Great Tooth Fairy Rip-Off.* Minneapolis: Fairview Press, 1997.

Carlson, Nancy. *I Like Me.* New York: The Trumpet Club, 1988.

Dr. Seuss. *ABC.* New York: Random House, 1963.

Dr. Seuss. *Green Eggs and Ham.* New York: Random House, 1960.

Children's Books No Home Should Be Without

Dr. Seuss. *Hop on Pop.* New York: Random House, 1963.

Dudko, Mary Ann, and Margie Larsen. *Barney's Color Surprise.* Allen, Texas: Lyrick Publishing, 1993.

Eastman, P. D. *Are You My Mother?* New York: Random House, 1960.

Eastman, P. D. *Go, Dog, Go!* New York: Random House, 1961.

Harris, Robie H. *Happy Birth Day!* Cambridge, Mass.: Candlewick Press, 1996.

Hill, Eric. *Spot's First Picnic.* New York: Putnam, 1987.

London, Jonathon. *Froggy Gets Dressed.* New York: Scholastic, 1992.

McBratney, Sam. *Guess How Much I Love You.* Cambridge, MA: Candlewick Press, 1994.

Melmed, Laura Krauss. *I Love You as Much . . .* New York: Lothrop, Lee, and Shepard Books, 1993.

Munsch, Robert. *Love You Forever.* New York: Firefly Books, 1986.

Numeroff, Laura Joffe. *If You Give a Mouse a Cookie.* New York: Harper and Row, 1985.

Schnetzler, Pattie. *Ten Little Dinosaurs.* Seattle: Accord Publishing, 1996.

Slim Goodbody. *The Body.* Minneapolis: Fairview Press, 1996.

Slim Goodbody. *The Mind.* Minneapolis: Fairview Press, 1996.

Slim Goodbody. *The Spirit.* Minneapolis: Fairview Press, 1996.

Slim Goodbody. *The Cycle of Life.* Minneapolis: Fairview Press, 1997.

Waber, Bernard. *Ira Sleeps Over.* Boston: Houghton Mifflin, 1972.

Wells, Rosemary. *Edward's Overwhelming Overnight.* New York: Dial Books for Young Readers, 1995.

White, Stephen. *Barney's Favorite Mother Goose Rhymes.* Allen, Texas: Lyrick Publishing, 1993.

Zion, Gene. *Harry the Dirty Dog.* New York: Harper and Row, 1956.

Children's Books No Home Should Be Without

Magazines for Children

Highlights for Children
P.O. Box 182167
Columbus, OH 43218-2167

Cricket
Carus Publishing Co.
315 Fifth St.
Peru, IL 61354

Sesame Street
Children's Television Workshop
P.O. Box 55518
Boulder, CO 80322-5518

First Step Math Series. Milwaukee: Gareth Stevens Publishing, 1994.

Helping Your Child Series. Washington, D.C.: U.S. Department of Education, Office of Educational Research and Improvement, 1993.

Keeshan, Bob. *Books to Grow By: Fun Children's Books Recommended by Bob Keeshan, TV's Captain Kangaroo.* Minneapolis: Fairview Press, 1995.

Keeshan, Bob. *Family Fun Activity Book: Playtimes and Activities to Bring Children and Grownups Together!* Minneapolis: Fairview Press, 1994.

Keeshan, Bob. *Holiday Fun Activity Book: Holiday Playtimes and Activities to Bring Children and Grownups Together!* Minneapolis: Fairview Press, 1995.

Spizman, Robyn Freedman. *Kids on Board: Fun Things to Do While Commuting or Road Tripping with Children.* Minneapolis: Fairview Press, 1997.

Usborne Parents' Guides. London: Usborne House, 1989.

Yeager, Mark. *Breakfast Is Only the Beginning: A Fun-Filled Guide to Keeping Up with Your Preschooler.* Minneapolis: Fairview Press, 1997.

Books for Parents